COLLECTOR'S
Toy
yearbook
IDENTIFICATION & VALUES

100 years of great toys

David Longest

COLLECTOR BOOKS
A Division of Schroeder Publishing Co., Inc.

Cover design by Beth Summers
Book design by Mary A. Hudson
Photography by Charles R. Lynch

Collector Books
P.O. Box 3009
Paducah, Kentucky 42002-3009

www.collectorbooks.com

Copyright © 2008 David Longest

The prices in this guide are derived by the author, wholly independent of the Walt Disney Company and The Walt Disney Company has not connection therewith. This book makes reference to "Mickey Mouse" and other various characters and films produced by the Walt Disney Company. All of the Disney characters and films are copyrighted by the Walt Disney Company. The characters also serve as trademarks of The Walt Disney Company.

The current values in this book should be used only as a guide. They are not intended to set prices, which vary from one section of the country to another. Auction prices as well as dealer prices vary greatly and are affected by condition as well as demand. Neither the author nor the publisher assumes responsibility for any losses that might be incurred as a result of consulting this guide.

Searching for a Publisher?

We are always looking for people knowledgeable within their fields. If you feel that there is a real need for a book on your collectible subject and have a large comprehensive collection, contact Collector Books.

Proudly printed and bound in the United States of America

Contents

Acknowledgments

This book marks a happy return for me to the world of antique toy writing. I would personally like to thank both Bill Schroeder and Billy Schroeder for their faith in my projects over the years. Back in 1983 when I was a relative novice to the collecting world with only a couple of national antique toy articles to my credit, they put their faith in me. Now, 24 years later, I have written six books on antique toys for Collector Books and have two new titles being released this year. For their support and encouragement, I will always be grateful.

I would also like to thank Gail Ashburn, editor, and Amy Sullivan, assistant editor, at Collector Books for the seemingly impossible and often thankless task of turning the stacks of hundreds of photos and layout pages into something that is now a book. Your work and designs are always amazing, and this author thanks you from the bottom of his heart for making him look good… and sometimes even intelligent.

In addition, I'd like to thank new friends and old who have helped make this year a most memorable one. To Doctors Dan Eichenberger, Mark Bickers, and Brian Ganzel… thanks for saving my life! Five by-passes later and 45 pounds less have made all the difference in the world! To Dale and Mendy Yost, thanks for taking care of all the little things one unfortunately forgets to do when you are rushed to a hospital and then they *keep you*! You have been true friends for life, and you never forget to show it. To Glenn Edwards, my friend forever, may our "Counting Cows" roadshow make it one of these years. And to my new friend in Disneyana, Brian Walker, may you carry on the Disneyana tradition for yet another generation.

To my wife, Ann, thanks for the prodding that kept me at my computer as deadlines approached and for the endless understanding that living with a toy collector means enduring the habits of a kid who never grew up. I am thankful that you have shared my hobby for the past 27 years of our marriage and put up with it even when we were dating as college kids. It was tempting to just sit on the floor and play with our golden retrievers all evening, but you always encouraged me to get back to the task at hand. No writer ever had a better coach, or wife. Mark Twain's wife Livvy did the very same thing. He may have done all the writing, but it was a steadfast wife who kept him on task and made sure he produced something. So, for all the great wives out there and personal coaches, I thank you. And I thank my own. Love you.

For Claire, my daughter, who is now a musical theatre student at Otterbein College in Columbus, Ohio, and the true inspiration of my seemingly crazed lunacy to write two books at once, may you watch your dad grow old gracefully surrounded by childhood playthings. Like Peter Pan, I just never grew up, and when your teenaged friends came to call and realized that your father was somehow a little "different," you were always gracious and understanding. I thank you for that. To my Mom, I'm glad you are still around to see yet another work of mine through to the end. Not sure why you kept all of my books over all these years except for the same reason any parent saves old baseball gloves, ice skates, trophies, artwork, and yes, old toys. Thanks for being there for me all these years.

Finally, to Elmer and Viola Reynolds of Martinsville, Indiana, thank you for your forever friendship. If I hadn't been shut out at that auction in rural Indiana some 26 years ago and you hadn't bid upon and won that huge old showcase that was far too large for any one person to carry down your basement stairs, we would never have met. And think of all the museum openings, antique shows, St. Charles Antique Toy World shows, Indianapolis Antique Advertising Shows, country auctions, flea markets, and evenings of "Show and Tell" that we would have missed together. Your collecting passions fueled my own, and after a quarter of a century, it's still fun to know that you are far more than friends could ever be, you are dear family. My books would not exist without your input, your knowledge, you enthusiasm, and yes, your fantastic toys. Thank you, thank you, thank you!

I would also like to thank the following persons, publications, and institutions who have helped educate me as a writer and a collector for over 30 years: Ted Hake, Tom Tumbusch, Michael Stern, George Hattersley, The Children's Museum of Indianapolis, William and Mary Furnish, Dave and Elaine Hughes, Terry Stewart and Stewart Promotions, Doug Moore and the Indianapolis Antique Advertising Show, Bob Coup, Herb Smith and Smith House Auctions, Dale Kelly and both *Antique Toy World Magazine* and Antique World Toy Shows, Keith and Donna Kaonis with *Collector's Showcase Magazine*, Kyle Husfloen and *Toy Shop Magazine*, *The Antique Trader* magazine, *The Tri-State Trader*, Indiana University and Indiana University Southeast, Dr. Richard Brengle, Bob Bernabe, Joe Reese, Helene and Stewart Pollack, Jim Miller,

Butch and Linda Miller, Jane Eberle, Harry and Jean Hall, Tommy Hall, Mel Birnkrandt, Maurice Sendak, Mike and Gina Sullivan, Bernie Shine, Steve Quertermous, Les Fish, Keith Spurgeon, Maxine and Stuart Evans, Andrea Evans, Brimfield Antique Shows of Brimfield, Massachusetts, and anybody else whom I might have forgotten.

And to collectors new to the world of toy collecting and those who have been at it for decades like myself, may we all never forget that these great old toys were once owned by children.

It's a unique forever-young and endearing endless childhood quest we have set out upon, and may that quest never end. Thanks to all who have helped make antique toy collecting what it is today.

David Longest,
February, 2007

Introduction

Welcome to the first edition of the *Collector's Toy Yearbook*. This book is intended to be a quick, easy-to-use reference regarding the collecting of antique and collectible toys in general for both the novice and the advanced collector. Our sample in this book is by no means exhaustive. In truth, the 100 years of toys that we present here are just a starting point. But the attempt is to give collectors a visual catalog of toys that are actually out there in the collecting world, what a collector might seriously expect to pay for them, and tips on building, maintaining, and sustaining a significant toy collection over the years.

Obviously, this book is for toy collectors. That is where the first half of the title comes in. But more importantly, the second half of the title gives the most important clue to this book's true use… it is a yearbook. It is a yearbook which attempts to group similar toys from similar time frames and put their values into perspective while giving even the new collector an idea of what is available to be collected and from what decades. In addition, it is a current yearbook which discusses "hot" trends in toy collecting from the immediate present and makes predictions as to where this whole fun and rewarding hobby is heading in the future.

The book is divided into sweeping chronological periods. The first chapter, Victorian and Golden Age Toys, looks at collectibles from 1900 through the beginning of the Depression in 1929. Although this does encompass the final years of Queen Victoria's reign, it is mainly the period in which toy mass production comes of age in America. Factories are actually built in this period which are devoted to nothing else than manufacturing great toys. This period also includes toys from one of America's most affluent times, often referred to as the jazz age. The second chapter introduces toys from The Thirties and the War, covering a period from 1930 through 1949. This chapter represents one of our largest samplings of toys as it includes both the vibrant comic and cartoon characters from the heyday of Hollywood (including Disney) combined with the wonderful toys associated with both the pre- and post WWII era. The third chapter contains this author's favorite toys titled T.V. Room and the Baby Boom covering toys from the 1950s through 1969. Why the favorite? The answer is simple: this author's childhood began in 1954 and carried on into the 1960s. These are the toy memories that will stir the hearts of any so-called baby boomer. Finally, Modern Toys visits a sizable sampling of toys from 1970 through the present, and makes strong predictions as to what will be the next hot collectibles in the toy collecting field.

The prices in this book are only a guide for the collector to use as a tool. Certainly all collectors pay different prices for the exact same toy at any given hour of any given day. Toy prices on the internet and at flea markets and toy shows are always determined by supply and demand on any given day. Other price factors include rarity of a toy, condition of a toy, the seller's willingness to sell a toy and the buyer's desire or even compulsion to buy it, the "mood" of the transaction between buyer and seller, and finally the geographical and economical region where the toy sale is taking place. Thus, any price guide such as this one has built-in errors from the start since its publication will reach an entire nation. Please use this book as just one more informative source upon which to base your own judgment. This isn't a price guide to end all price guides. It is simply an additional resource which will take the toy collector through 11 decades of toy manufacturing and hopefully educate him as to what is available to be collected in the vast collecting world and what he might expect to pay for a toy in order to have it added to his collection. Along the way as the reader takes this tour of 100 years of toys, it is the author's hope that this book will be valuable in pointing out what makes a toy collectible, what makes them valuable, what makes them rare, and how to tell the difference.

As collectors young and old make their way through these pages, it is my hope that the photographs and the information presented here will inspire yet another generation to continue to collect. The price guide presented throughout the photo captions is at best a general one. I have used the E/MV value code which breaks down to the first price listed being the current average value estimate for that particular toy pictured as found in excellent condition, and the second value listed is the value of the toy in today's collector marketplace as found in mint condition. If a toy is pictured with its original box, then assume the values relate to that toy in as-pictured condition, with its original box. If no original packaging or boxing is photographed, then assume the values are for the toy pictured without its box.

This pricing takes into account recent trends in antique toy collecting. Certainly the internet has made even extremely rare examples of antique toys easier to find with instant access, but with this immediacy comes what I regard as price volatility. Internet auction sites are useful, but sometimes very fickle when it comes to using prices realized at auction to establish true worth or value of a particular toy. A rare antique toy windup that sells for $2,000.00 on a given Tuesday night when no bidder out there seems to be at home or available to bid, might sell for $3,500.00 at prime time on a Saturday night closing sale when several competing bidders have discovered it. The fact that the same toy in the same condition might have sold with a comparative $1,500.00 value spread doesn't tell us that the toy's value has changed, it simply illustrates that in the collecting world, particularly among rare and antique toys (and this includes all categories), values are market driven. As always, it is immediate supply and demand. It's all a matter of how many people want a particular toy, and how much they are willing to pay for it.

So use this value guide with its intended purpose in mind. It is a guide. Don't use it to appraise your entire collection because too many variables compete for an exact appraisal of any given item. Use the prices and the ranges presented here for your own reference to gauge an approximate value of what a given toy might cost you today in the marketplace at either a specialized antique toy show or a competitive internet auction. It is this author's hope that you find you have acquired many of your toys at well below the market values presented here (known to us in the collecting world as "sleepers"), and may you find that many of your toys are worth exactly what you paid for them because you already knew that they had great value, rarity, and worth (known in the collecting world as "keepers").

In addition, this book will attempt to illustrate some common sense approaches to figuring out how old a particular toy is by its maker, its method of production, its material of production, its use, and its design. All of the factors are key indicators to identifying a toy's particular place in history.

Use this book as an introduction to toy collecting if you are a novice. Use it as another informative resource to add to your toy reference library if you are an advanced collector. Either way, use it in the spirit in which it was written — a common celebration for all of us who love the art of antique toys!

Since the beginnings of our nation, children have had toys. Look in early historical museums of America and one of the most interesting reflections of our nation's affluence is the way in which our children have enjoyed their free time. Colonial era children played early learning games with letters and the alphabet, and wooden folk dolls and lead toy soldiers still survive today. In the mid-1800s, photographic processes and lithography came into being and so another dimension was added to children's toys — realistic color. In Mark Twain's historical home at Nook Farm in what is today Hartford, Connecticut, he was blessed with three little girls and because of his great wealth, he showered them with wonderful toys in their nursery. These toys still survive today and are a testament to the fun-loving kind of father he was. Many of the surviving Matthew Brady formal photographs taken during the Civil War era show children with amazing antique toys which were once just contemporary playthings. The Margaret Strong Museum in Rochester, New York, is jammed to the gills with playthings from across America, from recent years all the way back to our founding fathers. Ms. Strong's toy collecting prowess and the scope of her now famous collection is matched only by the American ingenuity present in nearly 400 years of toy fabrication witnessed by the countless rows of thousands of toys. Toys are as American as baseball and apple pie!

Since the *Collector's Toy Yearbook* has sought to bear witness to the last century or so of American toy production, we decided to begin right at 1900. What was going on in 1900 that marks it as a hallmark year for toy production? Absolutely nothing. In truth, it's just a timetable watermark — a random point in time for discussion. What's more significant is what had gone on before we get to 1900. Specifically, the industrial revolution which brought about the changes of mass production, assembly lines, and rapid production combined with the invention of photographic processes and full-color lithography allowed factories to be built which would churn out children's books, puzzles, games, dolls, blocks, doll houses, tin tea sets, and even pull toys at a phenomenal rate. Like the printing press had made books and education possible for all centuries earlier, mass production and the lithographic process made toys affordable for all children whose parents produced enough income. If a family had any disposable income available after food and shelter, it is likely that there were at least a few toys in the house in 1900. So that is where our yearbook begins.

Major toys manufacturers of this period include several great early century giants whose company names are a staple among serious toy collectors today. McLoughlin Brothers began producing lithographed toys before the Civil War. They produced some of the most beautiful late 1800s and early 1900s children's picture books and story blocks. Several of them are shown in the pages of this chapter. Although it is not the most valuable toy pictured in this book, the toy dearest to my heart is pictured as the very first toy in the book. It's a Gong Bell pony wagon pull toy, circa 1890s, that belonged to my grandfather. Its dollar value is diminished by the missing gong bell but its sentimental value is heightened by the fact that I was the youngest of six grandchildren and darn lucky to have been the one kid in the farmhouse who couldn't put the toy down as a youngster. Subsequently, my grandmother gave it to me when I was in my 30s because I was the only "little one" she could ever remember who cared anything about it. Even as a toddler, I had excellent taste in antique toys! Gong Bell manufactured general use hardware bell items as a staple, but also manufactured some toys. The company was in production from 1886 through the 1930s, and it was my grandmother's belief that this toy was purchased for my grandfather, Ed Wells, around his fourth Christmas, in 1892. The toy was given to me in 1982, some 90 years later!

Another prominent toy manufacturing company during the 1900s was the Gibbs Manufacturing Company of Canton, Ohio, which began toy manufacturing in 1886. The company was first known for its production of plows, but branched into toys just two years after the founding of the company. Gibbs manufactured paper on wood and metal lithographed toys. A fine Gibbs horse-drawn wagon is pictured in this chapter.

The Rufus Bliss Company of Pawtucket, Rhode Island, produced toys from the 1830s through 1914. Some of the most desirable dollhouses ever produced were manufactured by Bliss just after the turn of the century. One such small example is also pictured in this chapter. Adding highly detailed lithographed paper labels to generally simple wood toys was an inexpensive and quick way to add color and desirability (not to mention, realism) to a toy. Both Gibbs Manufacturing and Bliss learned that this toy design method worked wonders. Early turn of the century lithographed paper and wood toys are some of the most desirable (and expensive) Victorian era toys available to today's collectors. These toys have stood the test of time for over a century, quite well in many cases. The only real enemies to beautiful Victorian paper and wood lithographed toys are excessive humidity (which hastens decomposition), insects (who love to feast on both old paper and the glue backing), and intense ultraviolet light (from direct sunlight) which tends to fade inks, especially tones of red, quickly. Collectors who plan to collect toys from this era need to make sure that toys are out of direct sunlight, behind reflective glass, protected from dust, and in a humidity-controlled environment. This sounds highly technical, but in truth, a regular showcase in a normally heated home works fine for all of the above, as long as the showcase doesn't face the direct sunlight.

Other fine antique toys from this period include tin windup tanks and transportation toys inspired by the real vehicles of World War I. Many of these feature highly colorful early lithography and wonderful windup actions. Additionally, the first appearance of the actual automobile occurs during this time period, so early renditions of the very earliest antique automobiles and tractors are pictured in this chapter in both tinplate and cast iron.

Kenton Hardware Company of Kenton, Ohio, manufactured wonderful cast iron horse drawn fire equipment, banks, and stoves beginning around 1890 and continuing until around 1952. The sturdy old cast iron horse drawn fire engines and wagons manufactured by Kenton, Ives, Arcade, and many other manufacturers have also lasted well over the past century, but collectors need to test the market by asking questions, reading cast iron specific toy guides, and surfing the internet to find out current trends and prices in this unusual area. One of the major negative factors facing collectors of cast iron toys today is the literal thousands of copies and reproductions that still flood the market annually. Cast iron fakes and unmarked reproductions are not the serious problem they were in the early 1980s when antique toy forgeries seemed to reach a zenith because of highly inflated toy prices, but reproductions are surfacing daily and being sold as authentic, often by dealers who don't know the difference. If a toy deal in cast iron seems too good to be true, and the price is far too low for a 100 year old toy, then the deal might be suspect. Arm yourself with knowledge. Before spending hundreds (even thousands of dollars) on cast iron toy sets, know the genre. Educate yourself. It's quite easy to allow weather to attack a reproduction toy and make it look old. It's an old wives' tale, but it works. Bury a "new" cast iron toy in the back yard and depending on the soil content, it

can look ancient in a few weeks. Know the dealer you are purchasing cast iron from, know the provenance (history) of the particular toy, and know your manufacturers. With these bits of knowledge, you will learn the beauty and joy of collecting cast iron toys.

This particular niche of toy collecting brings me a shudder every time I think about it. As mentioned earlier in this chapter, the Gong Bell horse pull toy in the very first photograph of this book was first owned by my grandfather. I have loved cast iron since I was a kid, but I am by no means an expert on it. About 12 years ago, I was asked to do a weekend-long presentation on antique toy collecting in general in the fine little Ohio town of Waynesville. I was their guest for a full weekend and at that time in the early 1990s had already written three or four books on collecting antique toys. I was by no means the expert on the subject, but I probably knew more than at least the average general line antique dealer. So I went to Waynesville to talk toys. (Note: This was long before the appearance of the popular show *Antiques Roadshow*, so even general antique dealers were eager to learn all they could about toys.) The Saturday afternoon Appraisal Day brought out a seemingly endless stream of collectors who brought their treasures into a presentation room set up much like a board meeting. I was a young expert on Disneyana, I knew transportation toys, character toys, Victorian toys, and children's books all quite well. But in regard to cast iron, I was weak and just learning. Now, picture this. The room not only contained collectors streaming into it, the board room table was filled with the fine dealers association representatives from the town who had hired me, which meant that my "bosses" were watching me too. (And I hadn't been paid my appearance stipend yet, either.) The first few collectors had toy cars, dolls, cap guns, character items…all toys under $300.00 each or so and I fired off appraisals with the swiftness and accuracy of a gunslinger. No problem. Then came a proud collector with three pristine, very long cardboard boxes. I was intrigued by the size and the condition of the boxes themselves, not knowing what they held, but from the weight of them in his arms, I figured it was my dreaded expert weakness — cast iron. I was less than an hour into the appraisal afternoon, and my credibility was about to be tested.

I seem to recall that the horse-drawn fire engines that he produced were by Kenton, maybe Ives. But they were a set of three, each about 24" long, looking like new, and for a moment, I thought maybe these were slick, new reproductions. I asked to see the boxes, which were pristine, and then examined the brown paper that was packed around each toy. No reproductions. These were the real thing! One was a very long pumper wagon drawn by a team of black horses, another was a fire wagon drawn by a white team, I believe, the third was a pristine ladder truck, also horse drawn. These were true museum pieces. I had never seen such wonderful cast iron examples, and certainly not a complete, boxed, matched set. Okay. I was about to be tested. I knew that he already knew what these were worth. And the rest of the antique dealers at the table knew that I knew that he knew. This was an appraisal chess game. Hmmmm. I knew, at that time, that pristine cast iron fire apparatus toys were worth in the thousands, and I had never seen even one example in a box. This guy had a very large, complete set of all three. My rationale was this: A single example of any of the three models he placed in front of me should bring $5,000.00 minimum at a specialized auction. The fact that he had all three added a considerable premium of at least 50% more to the price, and the boxes, although plain, added several more thousands. I asked how recent his last appraisal was, and I believe he answered "two months ago." And the location of the appraiser, I asked? New York was his answer. Okay, time for the gunslinger to fire a shot. I would bet that these could bring $27,000.00 as a complete boxed set at a good auction house, maybe more if the bidding got crazy. "And what was your recent appraisal?" He smiled, and showed me the paperwork, "$25,000.00" was his answer. The whole room breathed a sigh of relief. The young appraisal Billy the Kid had scored a bull's eye! The collector was happy because I had beat the earlier price by $2,000.00. The rest of the room was happy because they had hired me and had to sign my paycheck. I was happy because I had just made the most public educated guess of my life, and I was on the mark. I use this story to point out that appraisals and values are all relative. Even experts are sometimes just educated guessers. The only sure way to know what a toy is worth is to sell it, and even that may bring a purchase price that is over or under the toy's true worth. It is always a relative art. We want appraisals of toys, especially very valuable toys, to be totally scientific. But, in truth, toy values are always subjective. Prices and values are determined by who wants a toy, how many of them are available, how many others want it, and who wants it most.

Another fine toy manufacturer represented in this chapter is the Ernest Lehmann Company of Brandenburg, Germany. This company produced toys from the mid 1890s through 1929, although exports to the U.S. were limited during World War One. Many fine Lehmann examples are pictured in this chapter, and they represent the very finest quality in design, lithographed graphics, and windup clockwork function. The only drawback to collecting Lehmanns today is that they are quite expensive for the novice collector and although they are not fragile, they are extremely delicate. Collectors must take great care in preserving them as limbs of both animals and humans are usually very fragile tinplate that can dislodge from the design, break a metal tab, or totally fracture. They are beautiful, but these are rare because many couldn't last the test of time of multiple generations playing with them. Collectors of toys in the Victorian and pre-Depression eras can now prize playthings that now represent a time of an entire century gone by. Yes, the toys are works of art and design, and they are each a reflection of the people and machines of an era that will never be revisited, except through the eyes of the children of all ages who collect and play with them once again.

They are the true history of children who once lived, and the result of parents and family who once loved them enough to make sure they had toys, even when times were hard. Toys are a legacy of our leisure time and a testament to our love of fun.

Gong Bell Victorian pony cart pull toy, missing bell. Views of both sides shown. $600.00 – 1,000.00.

Victorian house by McLoughlin Brothers, paper, $100.00 – 200.00.

Victorian era Bliss doll house, 12" tall, opens in front, side views below. $1,400.00 – 2,000.00.

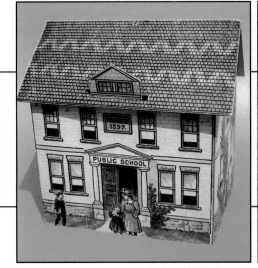

Early McLoughlin Brothers paper house, front and back views, $100.00 – 200.00.

Victorian McLoughlin Brothers paper house, gambrel roof, $100.00 – 200.00.

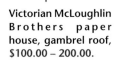

McLoughlin Brothers paper house, front and side view, 1900s, $100.00 – 200.00.

Victorian school house, paper, McLoughlin Brothers, side and back views, $100.00 – 200.00.

McLoughlin Brothers early 1900s paper house, side and back views $100.00 – 200.00.

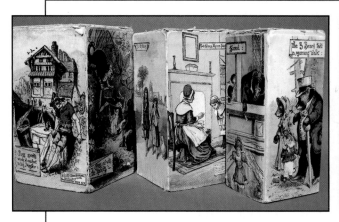

McLoughlin Brothers early blocks, nesting version, front, back, and sides shown. $500.00 – 800.00.

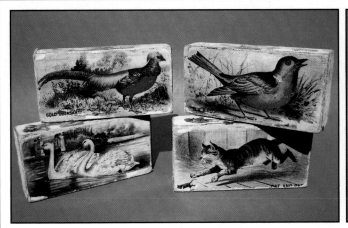

Set of four early Victorian picture blocks, front and reverse sides shown above, and side view, below. $200.00 – 300.00.

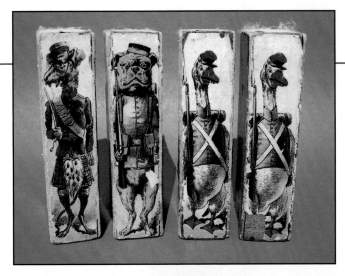

McLoughlin Brothers nesting Victorian blocks, set of three, different views. $300.00 – 500.00.

Three Victorian children's blocks, lithographed, front and back views. $150.00 – 300.00.

Set of three Buster Brown Victorian blocks, rare, front and side views. $300.00 – 500.00.

German tin windup dog and monkey, Lehmann, rare, $1,200.00 – 2,000.00.

German tin windup, lithographed, horse drawn clown, $600.00 – 850.00.

Harold Lloyd, tin windup character toy, 1920s, rare, $800.00 – 1,200.00.

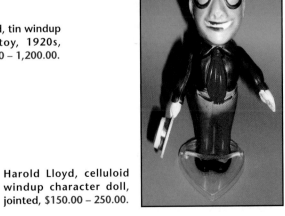

Harold Lloyd, celluloid windup character doll, jointed, $150.00 – 250.00.

Tutt Tutt, windup auto with driver, Lehmann, $1,800.00 – 3,000.00.

Moon Mullins and Kayo, windup handcar in original box, $2,000.00 – 3,000.00.

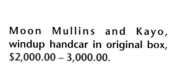

Tank with rubber tracks, tin windup, lithographed, $125.00 – 200.00.

Army Tank Number Three by Louis Marx, windup, $250.00 – 400.00.

Interstate bus, tin windup vehicle, 10" long, early, $350.00 – 550.00.

Green tractor with plow, tin windup, lithographed, $375.00 – 500.00.

Amos 'N' Andy fresh air taxi cab, windup, rare, $2,000.00 – 2,800.00.

The Powerful Katrinka tin windup toy, Fontaine Fox, 1923, $2,500.00 – 3,500.00.

Jazzbo Jim the Dancer on the Roof, by Unique Art, tin windup, $1,500.00 – 2,500.00.

Tiny Victorian pull toy, cloth dog on wheels, 4" tall, $500.00 – 800.00.

Pony cart manufactured by Gibbs, 1900s, $400.00 – 700.00.

Horse and sulkey, cast iron, early, $500.00 – 800.00.

Tractor, with giant white tires, cast iron, early, $300.00 – 450.00.

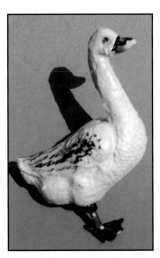

Large red tractor with metal tires, cast iron, $300.00 – 400.00.

Iron toy goose, early, 3" tall, $75.00 – 125.00.

Dual rider early friction auto, cast iron, rare, $1,000.00 – 1,500.00.

Toonerville Trolley tin windup, rare, with jointed driver, $1,000.00 – 1,500.00.

Touring sedan, cast iron, 8" long, $600.00 – 900.00.

Pennsylvania Railroad cast iron train car, rolls, $250.00 – 400.00.

Barney Google and Spark Plug game, Milton Bradley, 1923, $200.00 – 375.00.

Spark Plug painted wood roll toy, $300.00 – 450.00.

Spark Plug, jointed horse with blanket, by Schoenhut, $700.00 – 1,000.00.

Barney Google and Spark Plug, tin windup, rare, $2,000.00 – 3,500.00.

Rooster cast iron still bank, early, $225.00 – 350.00.

Turkey cast iron still bank, original paint, $250.00 – 350.00.

Cow cast iron still bank, original finish, $175.00 – 250.00.

Golden pig cast iron still bank, mint, $250.00 – 325.00.

Blue donkey cast iron still bank, $200.00 – 325.00.

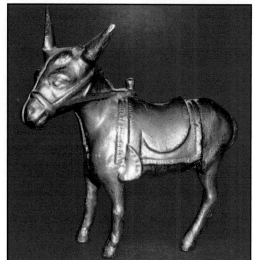

Rescue dog cast iron bank, rare and early, $300.00 – 475.00.

Boxer still bank, early with original finish, $200.00 – 300.00.

Prancing horse cast iron still bank, $200.00 – 300.00.

Camel cast iron still bank, near mint, early, $250.00 – 350.00.

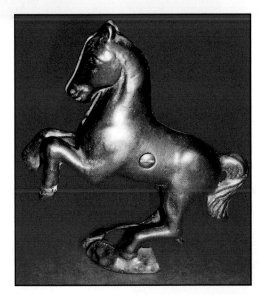

Prancing horse still bank, 6" tall, early, $225.00 – 300.00.

Red Goose Shoes cast iron still goose bank, $175.00 – 325.00.

Seated bear cast iron still bank, $250.00 – 350.00.

Clown cast iron still bank, gold and red paint, $200.00 – 300.00.

Elephant on drum cast iron still bank, original paint, $225.00 – 325.00.

Elephant cast iron still bank, with original paint, 5" tall, $235.00 – 375.00.

Large golden elephant cast iron still bank, 6" long, $250.00 – 375.00.

Radio bank, cast iron, with combination lock and opening door, $300.00 – 450.00.

Black man, soldier or scout, still bank, unusual, $300.00 – 400.00.

Boy Scout, WWI era, cast iron still bank, $200.00 – 350.00.

Mutt and Jeff cast iron still bank, early, $300.00 – 500.00.

Billikin red cast iron still bank, unusual, $200.00 – 325.00.

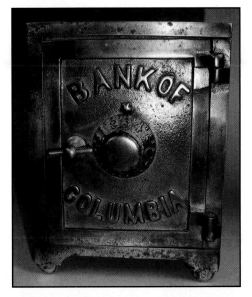

Bank of Columbia cast iron safe bank, early, $300.00 – 450.00.

General Electric early refrigerator bank, $300.00 – 450.00.

Victorian child's watering can, 1900s, rare, $500.00 – 800.00.

Tin sand pail with children playing, 8" tall, front and back views, $200.00 – 400.00.

Victorian tin pail by Amsco, rare
and early, $1,000.00 – 1,500.00.

Child's tin sand sifter with molds inside, lithographed, inside and side views, $100.00 – 175.00.

Victorian tea tray with dancing children, $175.00 – 300.00.

Child's tin lunch box, lithographed, $150.00 – 300.00.

Mary Had A Little Lamb tea set tray, $200.00 – 400.00.

Victorian tea set tray with two children, $150.00 – 250.00.

Mary Had A Little Lamb Victorian
tea plate, $75.00 – 125.00.

Victorian child's tea cup, embossed and lithographed, front and back views, $125.00 – 175.00.

Two early Victorian child's tea cups, $200.00 – 400.00.

Early Victorian china tea set, 1900s, mint condition. Close-up detail of cup, right. $500.00 – 800.00.

Victorian china cream pitcher, children with snowman, $200.00 – 300.00.

Three Little Bears china cream pitcher, front and back views, rare, $200.00 – 300.00.

Victorian doll house table complete with china tea set, $200.00 – 300.00.

Victorian doll house table with children's design, $125.00 – 200.00.

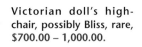

Victorian doll's high-chair, possibly Bliss, rare, $700.00 – 1,000.00.

Celluloid baby with swim ring, 5" tall, jointed, $125.00 – 200.00.

Little boy in swimming suit, celluloid figural doll, $125.00 – 200.00.

Buster Brown, celluloid jointed doll, 4" tall, $250.00 – 350.00.

Little maid celluloid doll, 6" tall, 1920s, $125.00 – 200.00.

Groom bisque doll with crepe paper clothes, 1920s, $150.00 – 250.00.

Flapper era bisque doll, companion to groom, $125.00 – 200.00.

Keystone Cop celluloid jointed doll, 5" tall, $200.00 – 300.00.

Skippy celluloid doll, 1920s, 6", jointed, $200.00 – 350.00.

Mutt and Jeff celluloid dolls, pair, $200.00 – 350.00.

Gentleman doll, possibly Charlie McCarthy, celluloid, $150.00 – 225.00.

Charlie Chaplin celluloid doll figure, 1920s, $150.00 – 250.00.

Jackie Coogan, Hollywood child star, celluloid doll, $200.00 – 300.00.

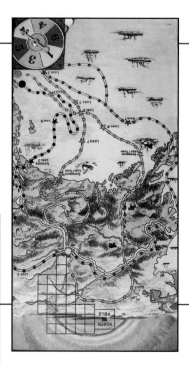

Game of to the North Pole by Air Ship, Milton Bradley, rare, with views of box detail and inside gameboard. $1,000.00 – 1,500.00.

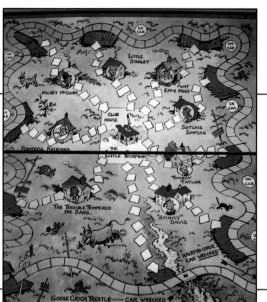

Toonerville Trolley game, Fontaine Fox, 1920s, with detail of game board at right. $250.00 – 400.00.

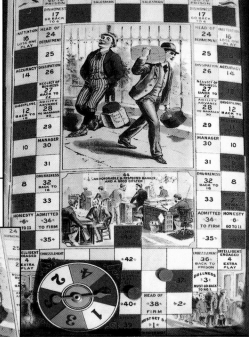

Game of the District Messenger Boy, early and rare, with details of box graphics. $300.00 – 500.00.

Little cloth German bear with glass eyes, rare, $200.00 – 350.00.

Early teddy bear, actual date unknown, worn, $200.00 – 350.00.

McLoughlin Brothers *Girls and Boys Come Out to Play*, 1901, $125.00 – 200.00.

McLoughlin Brothers *Little Housekeeper and Other Stories* book, 1904, $125.00 – 200.00.

Little Folks Story Book, 1900s, $125.00 – 175.00.

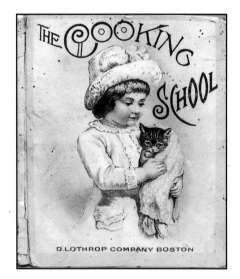

The Cooking School by D. Lothrop Company, Boston, $75.00 – 125.00.

Little Chatterers, Victorian, McLoughlin Brothers, $125.00 – 175.00.

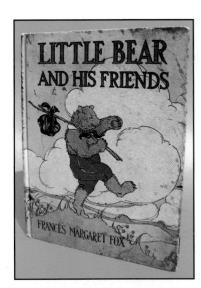

Pleasant Hours Painting Book, Father Tuck Series, 1900s, detail of pages above. $150.00 – 250.00.

Little Bear and His Friends, Frances Fox, $50.00 – 75.00.

Puss in Boots, published by Saalfield, $100.00 – 150.00.

Baby's Garden of Story and Rhyme, circa 1915, $125.00 – 175.00.

Fairy Tale Drawing Book, miniature size, 5", early, $125.00 – 175.00.

Little Red Riding Hood, Hurst and Company, New York, $125.00 – 200.00.

Little Red Riding Hood Star Rhymes, small book, 1900s, cover and color inside details, $135.00 – 175.00.

Little Red Riding Hood Story Cards, $25.00 – 50.00 each.

Little Red Riding Hood story book, color illustrated, $125.00 – 200.00.

Little Red Riding Hood "Aunt Kate Series,"
McLoughlin Brothers, $150.00 – 300.00.

Little Red Riding Hood, Raphael Tuck and Sons, rare book, $250.00 – 400.00.

Game of Little Red Riding Hood by Clark and Sowdon, 4" long, $200.00 – 300.00.

Little Red Riding Hood tea set, early, $250.00 – 350.00.

Little Red Riding Hood early tin tea set, selected pieces, $300.00 – 450.00.

Little Red Riding Hood set of three tin tea plates, $100.00 – 150.00.

Little Red Riding Hood meeting the wolf tin tea tray, rare, $250.00 – 400.00.

Little Red Riding Hood tea tray, 1920s, $35.00 – 60.00.

Child's Victorian piano, manufactured by Schoenhut, $250.00 – 350.00.

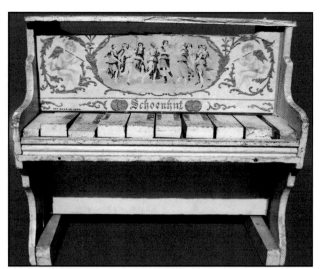

Harold Teen ukelele, decal, rare, 1920s, $500.00 – 750.00.

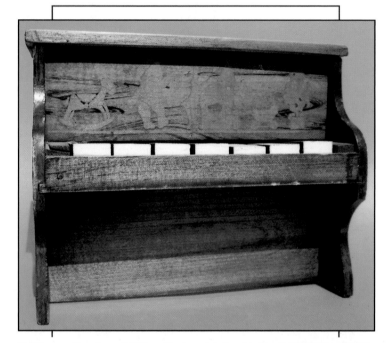

Child's wooden piano, 1920s, with close-up of gold stencil, $200.00 – 300.00.

Detail of character decal.

Happy Hooligan antique chalkware characters, 1900s, $600.00 – 950.00 pair.

Skeezix decorated box and dog napkin ring, $150.00 – 250.00.

Maggie from Maggie and Jiggs, giant bisque statue 7", $200.00 – 300.00.

Buster Brown mechanical valentine, 1900s $125.00 – 175.00.

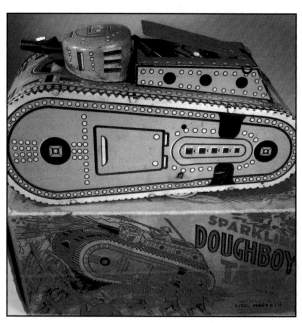

Sparkling Doughboy tank by Louis Marx, in original box, $350.00 – 600.00.

The Thirties and the War Years

The decades of the 1930s and the 1940s saw major changes on the American home front. Aside from being a rebounding decade where we dug ourselves out of the Great Depression, we as a nation also learned that although times had been hard in the recent past, they had been very, very good in the Roaring Twenties. And as the American economy rebounded and rebuilt after the Depression and as we headed into the decade of the 1940s and WW II, one lesson that we took with us was that it's never too gloomy to spoil our children. So, spoil we did. Partly because the age of invention and innovation brought about during the 1900s had given Americans such a wonderful introduction into the fun of leisure hours combined with a building of wealth among the labor force, and partially because toy manufacturers could hardly meet the demands of parents who made a choice to put fun toys in the hands of their beloved children, little ones growing up in the 1930s and 1940s had a wealth of toys to choose from.

Certainly the advent of radio and the importance of characters introduced on the air waves brought a significant influx of character merchandise to the toy store shelves. Little Orphan Annie was never more popular in the dime stores than the next day after her weekly broadcasts when the kids had money to burn and Woolworth's was just around the corner. Many fine examples of Little Orphan Annie toys are pictured in this chapter.

Comic strip toys first appeared in the 1900s with the birth of Richard Outcault's famous Yellow Kid and Buster Brown series, followed later by the Katzenjammer Kids, Toonerville Trolley, and many others. All of these comic strips inspired wonderful character merchandising spin-offs, and comic strip artists and syndicates alike soon realized that there was big money to be made in character licensing far beyond simple royalties which newspapers paid for comic strip art. This trend flourished in the 1930s and 1940s with such popular strips as Dick Tracy, Barney Google, Popeye, and a virtual host of Walt Disney created characters inspired by his early comic strip and movie characters. These character toys represent a significant sample of toy designs in this particular chapter, but they are only one impressive segment of these two very special decades in toy mass production.

Before we move away from the character toy influences of this period, collectors should look closely at the tremendous bargains they may be passing up daily on the internet and at toy shows and auctions. I have been a toy collector for more than 33 years (I started when I was 19) and I am old enough now to have witnessed the "fall from grace" of many once wonderfully collectible old toys. There is certainly nothing wrong with the toys themselves, but few young buyers or collectors today have any real childhood connection with the likes of Barney Google, Spark Plug, the Katzenjammer Kids, Buster Brown, or even Edgar Bergen and his mouthy alter ego, Charlie McCarthy. Mention to young collectors today the name Candice Bergen, and they know her television work… but most people under 40 have not a clue that her father was a famous radio performer and personality and that her younger little "dummy" brother (Charlie McCarthy) was once a hugely popular radio personality with a weekly show which spun off mass media publications and wonderful toy merchandising. Poor Charlie has been lost to time. His 15 minutes of fame have come and gone, and so have his toy values. Why? Who is still out there in the toy collecting world that even knows who Charlie is, and who cares about collecting him? Far fewer people than once did, thus, his toy prices are on the slide. And just as hedging bets and trends in the stock market can net profits, it works the same way in toys. Although Charlie McCarthy and the Toonerville Trolley gang may not be widely recognizable among young people, they all still hold an important place in the history of our popular culture. And these toys will always be desired by collectors of pop culture and general toy collectors who want broad samples of toys based upon important popular characters of another day. So, my advice is don't only buy what you recognize and what you like if your goal is an expansive collection of toys that represents both history and education. Your recognition of one of the "good old toys" might just net you a real bargain unrecognized by others. Remember the case of Charlie McCarthy. Let him be your standard.

This chapter also contains several examples of vintage 1930s Disneyana. Walt Disney's characters have never sunk into any pop culture oblivion because they are so exposed to every generation. Children of today who missed being exposed to 1930s pie-eyed Mickey Mouse through short films in the movie theatres now remember him from growing up with his cartoons on the cable Disney channel and the old Mickey cartoons pulled from the segments known as The Disney Vault. And the Walt Disney Company daily exhibits mastery in blending the old and the new. Visitors to Disney World today are greeted with all of the recognizable characters from the cartoons and feature films of the past 70 years, including Clarabelle Cow and Horace Horsecollar. Now, why would Disney have Clarabelle and Horace greeting visitors at an entrance when they each haven't appeared in a new movie in likely 75 years? Two reasons: nostalgia and recognition. Horace and Clarabelle proudly represent Walt's beginnings at the studio since these characters appear in the very earliest Disney films of the early 1930s. That's the nostalgia. These characters are currently featured in Disney's Family Fun Parade that appears daily at the Magic Kingdom. They give the parade the "Old Main Street" feel of warmth and good times past. But including them as greeters out front ensures that those characters will now be recognized by yet another generation of youngsters, 75 years after their inception! Nostalgia and recognition have allowed Disney to keep its characters, movies, and parks relevant while never changing too much. And that is why the Disney character toys of the 1930s and 1940s as pictured in this chapter will never lose their value. They are still present in the immediate popular culture. (Fans of Disneyana in general should seek out my newest work on Disney character merchandise, *Collecting Disneyana*, also published in the fall of 2007.)

This chapter also shows examples of toys inspired by World War II and transportation toys modeled after popular vehicles, tractors, transportation examples, airplanes, and automobiles of the time. Toy production materials prevalent during these two decades are tinplate and limited cast iron, early plastic, metal and pot metal, organic rubber, but nearly no wood. Natural rubber (durable and didn't cause scratches to kids or furniture) and lightweight celluloid (a natural blend of camphor and other chemicals which was a predecessor to modern plastics) were the toy production materials that flourished during the 1930s and 1940s. Celluloid toys were fragile, lightweight, safe, but very brittle. They could and did crack like an egg under use. They were also extremely inexpensive to manufacture. Many examples are pictured in this chapter. Notice the wonderful molded designs and warmth of the applied paints. Celluloid toy production relatively ceased in the years following World War II because more durable and equally safe and inexpensive modern plastics began to be discovered and used in toy production.

Today's collectors of toys from the 1940s should not overlook the historical impact of World War II upon children's collectibles. Imagine the value of toys from the Civil War period if they were available today (and, in essence, they are not). Toys associated with major events in history are always highly collectible and valuable, and playthings from the early to mid-1940s are still available at reasonable prices. Marx tanks, Hubley vehicles, Smith Miller (Smitty) trucks, Manoil Manufacturing toy soldiers — all of these were widely available through the Sears Roebuck catalog and so their distribution went far and wide. Toys of this period are still discovered regularly at farm and country auctions and flea markets. Buy them if you can at reasonable prices. These war related pieces of history are eventual money in the bank. And the prices for these are generally still quite reasonable.

The toys of the 1930s and the 1940s received wide distribution through catalog orders and local dime store chains such as Woolworth's. This wide distribution ensures that many fine examples still exist today, so much so that collectors can be discriminating regarding condition. If you buy for investment, demand excellent to mint examples without exception. Buying toys in less than desirable condition only serves to ensure that you will eventually have to sell off your "junk" and upgrade. Buy mint and you buy once. And you can take that advice to the bank.

Aside from Louis Marx, other fine companies who manufactured toys from this period are J. Chein, Fisher Price, N.N. Hill Brass, Manoil Manufacturing, Ohio Art, Marks Brothers of Boston, Unique Art, Knickerbocker Toys, Ideal Toy and Novelty, Lindstrom, and Courtland to name only a few.

Toys from the 1930s and 1940s belong in every serious toy collector's collection. This time period in history saw tremendous growth in manufacturing techniques, safety considerations, colorful lithographic printing, packaging, and clever design among American toys. Fine examples from these two decades can be an interesting backbone to a substantial serious collection. And the prices of toys from this period are still a bargain to this day!

Skeezix, oilcloth doll, 14",
$125.00 – 200.00.

Little Orphan Annie doll in original box, $750.00 – 1,000.00.

Little Orphan Annie dexterity palm puzzle, under glass, $150.00 – 200.00.

Radio Orphan Annie's Secret Society 1936, $125.00 – 150.00.

Radio Orphan Annie's, Secret Society 1938, $125.00 – 150.00.

Movie Komics box of filmstrips, Orphan Annie, Dick Tracy, etc., $75.00 – 100.00.

Little Orphan Annie and Sandy tin windup, $1,200.00 – 2,000.00 pair.

Little Orphan Annie clothes pins set, rare, $200.00 – 350.00.

Little Orphan Annie, metal stove with lithographed plates, $200.00 – 350.00.

Little Orphan Annie, stove, $150.00 – 300.00.

Little Orphan Annie Ovaltine plastic cups, set of three, $175.00 – 225.00.

Little Orphan Annie ceramic premium mug, $65.00 – 95.00.

Little Orphan Annie Ovaltine shakeup mug, premium, $65.00 – 100.00.

Captain Midnight Ovaltine mug, premium, $75.00 – 125.00.

Little Red Riding Hood, tea tray, 1930s, $150.00 – 225.00.

Noah's Ark (Disney copyright) giant tin pail, $300.00 – 400.00.

Chein mechanical coin bank, tin, lithographed, $200.00 – 350.00.

Billiken bank, cast iron, 4" tall, $125.00 – 250.00.

Modern refrigerator still bank, $200.00 – 325.00.

Elephant cast iron still bank, $200.00 – 300.00.

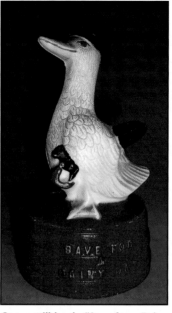

Goose still bank, "Save for a Rainy Day," $150.00 – 225.00.

Kitten cast iron still bank, original paint, $225.00 – 350.00.

Fido, little black dog, still bank, $150.00 – 200.00.

Scottie dog still bank, cast iron, $200.00 – 325.00.

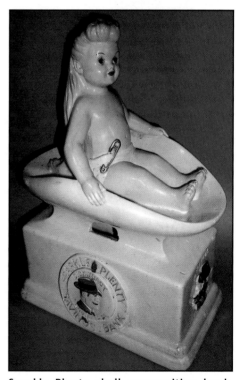

Sparkle Plenty chalk composition bank, extremely rare, $1,000.00 – 1,500.00.

Andy Panda tin lithographed book bank, Walter Lantz, $125.00 – 200.00.

Game of Alley Oop, Royal Toy Company, $100.00 – 150.00.

Pin the Tail on the Donkey game, $50.00 – 75.00.

Play Golf tin lithographed action game, by Ferdinand Strauss, $600.00 – 900.00.

Carousel giant metal windup, spinning action, $1,000.00 – 1,350.00.

Bunny windup cart, celluloid, 7" tall, $150.00 – 250.00.

Pig tin windup, by J. Chein, mint example, $125.00 – 175.00.

Turtle with rider tin windup toy, $200.00 – 300.00.

Li'l Abner Dog Patch Band windup, by Unique Art Manufacturing, $700.00 – 1,000.00.

Sunny Andy Fun Fair windup toy, $350.00 – 450.00.

Sunny Andy Kiddie Kampers windup toy, $350.00 – 450.00.

Windup monkeys and clown, Schuco of Germany, set of three, $750.00 – 1,250.00.

Bumper car, with detailed driver and rider, tin windup, $200.00 – 300.00.

Tin windup car with "balloon" tires, Marx, $300.00 – 500.00.

Old Jalopy action toy, lithographed tin windup, $300.00 – 500.00.

Marx motorcycle rider with working siren, windup, $300.00 – 500.00.

Donkey and mule driver windup toy, lithographed, $200.00 – 300.00.

Toylands Farm Products wagon, lithographed tin windup, $500.00 – 750.00.

Handcar windup, tin lithographed, by Girard, $500.00 – 700.00.

Hot dog vendor tin and plastic windup, $125.00 – 200.00.

Whoopie car tin windup, Louis Marx Company, 1930s, $450.00 – 700.00.

Milton Berle crazy car tin windup, by Louis Marx, $450.00 – 700.00.

Uncle Wiggily tin windup car, ca. 1935, Howard R. Garis, $800.00 – 1,250.00.

Goose tin windup action toy, lithographed, $300.00 – 400.00.

Duck tin windup, 4" tall, by J. Chein, $125.00 – 175.00.

Walking elephant tin windup, lithographed metal, $150.00 – 300.00.

Jumbo windup elephant, tin lithographed, $300.00 – 500.00.

Cat with ball windup, push tail lever action, by Marx, $300.00 – 400.00.

Alligator lithographed tin windup, 14" long, $200.00 – 375.00.

Drum Major #27 by Wolverine, giant windup, $700.00 – 1,000.00.

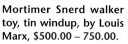

Mortimer Snerd walker toy, tin windup, by Louis Marx, $500.00 – 750.00.

Happy Holligan tin windup, lithographed, $500.00 – 750.00.

Red cap porter tin windup, 1930s, $300.00 – 550.00.

Joe Penner and His Duck Goo Goo tin windup toy, $500.00 – 750.00.

G.I. Joe jet propelled windup car, $400.00 – 600.00.

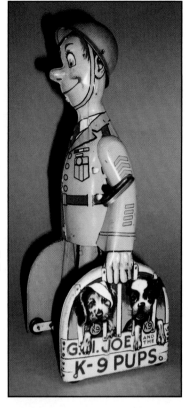

G.I. Joe and the K-9 Pups tin windup toy, by Unique Art, $300.00 – 475.00.

Silver windup airplane, marked D.R.G.M., $225.00 – 300.00.

Coast Defense gunner action toy, tin windup, lithographed, $275.00 – 400.00.

Super M 2 tin windup tank, lithographed, $250.00 – 350.00.

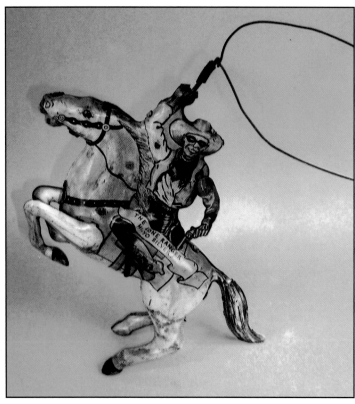

The Lone Ranger tin windup, lithographed, $750.00 – 1,000.00.

Buttercup windup, from Buttercup and Spare Ribs Comics, $700.00 – 1,000.00.

Girl on skis windup, lithographed tin, $200.00 – 300.00.

Knock Out Prize Fighters tin and wood windup, Ferdinand Strauss, ca. 1921, $900.00 – 1,300.00.

Fire Chief Siren Coupe, working siren, by Girard, $600.00 – 900.00.

Metal race cars, 4" long, white balloon rubber tires, $100.00 – 200.00.

Auburn Toys racer, 7" long, $75.00 – 100.00.

Red rubber racer, by Auburn, 1930s, $125.00 – 200.00.

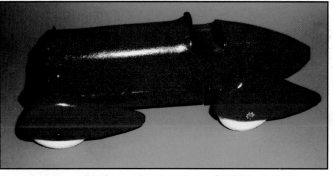

Red streamlined racer, by Wyandotte, $200.00 – 350.00.

Hubley Hook and Ladder Truck, in original box, $300.00 – 450.00.

H.J. Heinz pickle truck, Metal Craft of St. Louis, $600.00 – 900.00.

Red dump truck with working dump bed, by Metal Masters, $150.00 – 250.00.

Ambulance by Wyandotte Toys, $200.00 – 350.00.

Century of Progress Greyhound Bus, white tires, $300.00 – 500.00.

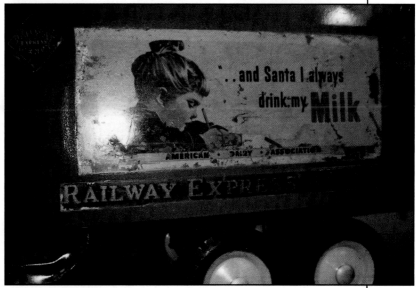

Buddy L Railway Express truck,
repainted, $500.00 – 850.00.

Army vehicles, selection of five, pot metal, 1940s, $250.00 – 400.00.

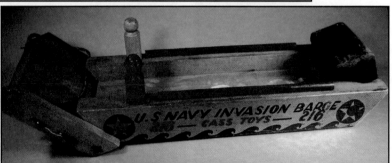

U.S. Navy Invasion Barge, wooden, Cass Toys, 1940s, $150.00 – 250.00.

Large metal plane, by Hubley Kiddie Toy, $200.00 – 350.00.

John Deere tractor, Arcade, extremely rare version, $1,200.00 – 1,800.00.

Metal pistol with Lone Ranger
decal, $250.00 – 400.00.

Coast Defense Gun, boxed
set #830, $275.00 – 400.00.

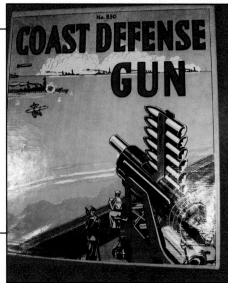

Army figures with metal hats,
set of eleven, $300.00 – 450.00.

Army soldier,
Dimestore type,
with silver metal
hat, $35.00 – 65.00.

Army soldier, Dimestore
type, rare version,
$25.00 – 45.00.

Superman Krypto Raygun, in original
box with films, $1,200.00 – 2,000.00.

Flash Gordon
Target Games,
lithographed
metal set,
$200.00 – 350.00.

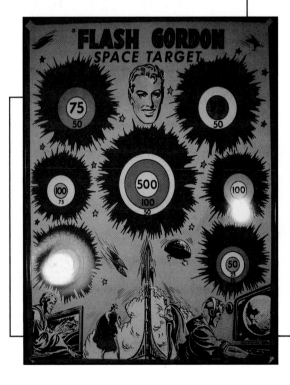

Flash Gordon Space-Outfit, in box, by Esquire Novelty, $400.00 – 750.00.

Flash Gordon Sonic Blaster, rare air shooting toy, $750.00 – 1,000.00.

Flash Gordon Rocket Fighter tin sparking windup, $800.00 – 1,200.00.

Red Ryder Target Game, in
original box, $500.00 – 750.00.

Red Ryder boxed bagatelle game,
by Gotsam Steel, $500.00 – 800.00.

Red Ryder frame tray puzzle, mint, $125.00 – 200.00.

Red Ryder Gun and Holster set, by Daisy, $400.00 – 650.00.

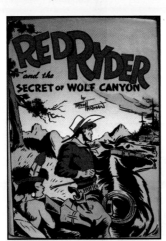

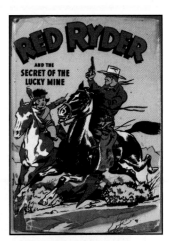

Red Ryder and the Mystery of Whispering Walls, by Harman, $75.00 – 100.00.

Red Ryder and the Secret of Wolf Canyon, by Fred Harman, $75.00 – 100.00.

Red Ryder and the Adventure of Chimney Rock, by Harman, $75.00 – 100.00.

Red Ryder and the Secret of the Lucky Mine, by Harman, $75.00 – 100.00.

Tom Mix Circus Game,
by Parker Brothers,
$200.00 – 300.00.

Tom Mix and the Scourge of Paradise Valley Big Big Book, by Whitman Publishing, $125.00 – 150.00.

Tom Mix, cowboy boots
box, $200.00 – 300.00.

Charlie McCarthy wood composition bank, rare, $250.00 – 350.00.

Charlie McCarthy doll, wood composition, 12" tall, $300.00 – 400.00.

Charlie McCarthy walker toy, tin windup, by Marx, $600.00 – 800.00.

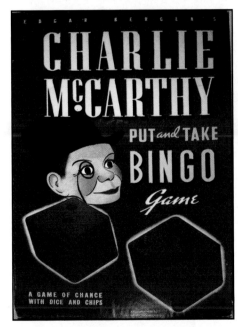

Charlie McCarthy Put and Take Bingo Game, by Whitman Publishing, $200.00 – 300.00.

Charlie McCarthy Benzine Buggy windup, Marx, $1,000.00 – 1,300.00.

Dick Tracy Siren Pistol, metal construction with decal, $200.00 – 300.00.

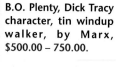

Dick Tracy Military Set child's brush, $35.00 – 65.00.

Dick Tracy Target dart set, Famous Artists Syndicate, $200.00 – 300.00.

B.O. Plenty, Dick Tracy character, tin windup walker, by Marx, $500.00 – 750.00.

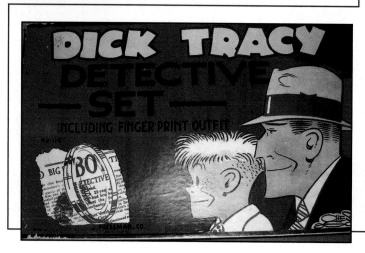

Dick Tracy Detective Set, by J. Pressman, $300.00 – 450.00.

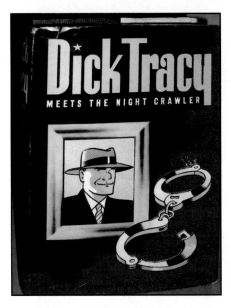

Dick Tracy Meets the Night Crawler,
$75.00 – 100.00.

Uncle Wiggily Goes Camping,
$50.00 – 75.00.

America in Action patriotic play book,
1940s, $100.00 – 150.00.

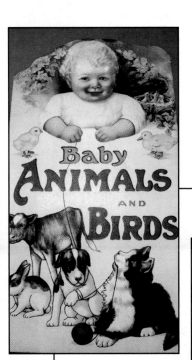

Baby Animals and Birds, child's
storybook, $125.00 – 165.00.

Buffalo Bill Wild West Annual, illustrated,
$75.00 – 125.00.

Tom Sawyer Painting Set, based upon the movie, $125.00 – 200.00.

Skippy Paint and Coloring Set, $250.00 – 350.00.

Popeye Paints, lithographed tin box, ca. 1933, $70.00 – 100.00.

Popeye boxed chalk set, by American Crayon, 1936, $75.00 – 125.00.

Popeye boxed chalk set, by American Crayon, 1936, $75.00 – 125.00.

Popeye white chalk, in original box, $65.00 – 100.00.

Popeye palm puzzle game, under glass, $125.00 – 200.00.

Popeye Playing Card Game, by Whitman, $75.00 – 150.00.

Popeye figural filament bulb and rare lamp, $1,000.00 – 1,800.00.

Popeye Cheers Christmas lamp covers in original lithograph box, $150.00 – 300.00.

Popeye Express tin windup toy with parrot cage, by Marx, $1,000.00 – 1,500.00.

Popeye squeak toy, by Rempel Manufacturing Company, $150.00 – 200.00.

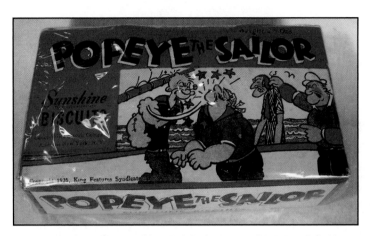

Popeye the Sailor Sunshine Biscuits box, rare, $200.00 – 350.00.

Popeye and Olive Oyl roof dancers tin windup toy, $1200.00 – 2,000.00.

Popeye the pilot tin windup airplane, 1930s, rare, $1200.00 – 1,800.00.

Popeye Bubble set, appears complete, $200.00 – 300.00.

Popeye Pipe Toss Game, copyright King Features, complete, $250.00 – 350.00.

Popeye Playing Card Game in original box, ca. King Features Syndicate, $125.00 – 200.00.

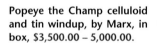

Popeye the Champ celluloid and tin windup, by Marx, in box, $3,500.00 – 5,000.00.

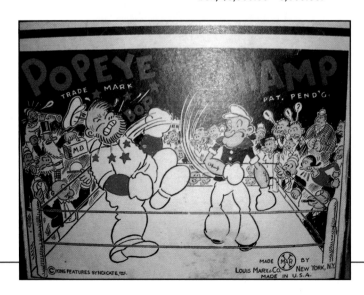

Popeye alarm clock with lithographed art all over, rare, $1,000.00 – 1,500.00.

Wimpy squeak toy, by Rempel Manufacturing Company, $150.00 – 200.00.

Olive Oyl push toy, Olive Oyl being kidnapped, rare, $600.00 – 900.00.

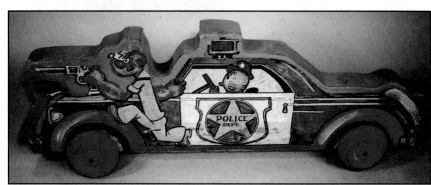

Popeye police dept. lithographed paper on wood car, rare, $700.00 – 1,000.00.

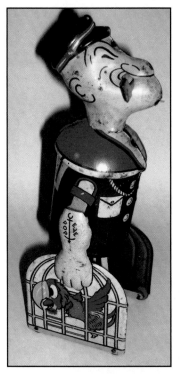

Popeye with parrot cages tin windup toy, 1930s, $700.00 – 1,000.00.

Olive Oyl squeak toy, by Rempel Manufacturing Company, $150.00 – 200.00.

Barnacle Bill the sailor, similar to Popeye design, tin windup, $400.00 – 750.00.

Mickey Mouse, Minnie Mouse, and Long-billed Donald toothpick holders, set of all three, rare, $2,000.00 – 3,000.00.

Mickey Mouse lead figure, 4" tall, probably German, rare, $1,000.00 – 1,500.00.

Mickey Mouse figural celluloid doll, 8", 1930s, $1,000.00 – 1,750.00.

Mickey Mouse and Donald Duck nodder composition banks. $300.00 – 500.00 each.

Mickey Mouse lamp base, chalkware, by Soreng-Mangold, $1,000.00 – 1,500.00.

Mickey and Minnie Mouse dolls by Nifty, rare pair, $3,000.00 – 4,000.00.

Mickey Mouse doll, by Steiff of Germany, 7" tall, 1930s, $750.00–1,200.00.

Mickey Mouse doll, by Knickerbocker Toy Company, $400.00 – 700.00.

Mickey Mouse jointed doll, wood composition, 12", rare, $750.00 – 1,100.00.

Mickey and Minnie tea tray, 1930s, $150.00 – 250.00.

Mickey Mouse tin child's tea set tray, Ohio Art, 1930s, $200.00 – 300.00.

Mickey Mouse tin tea tray, Ohio Art, 1930s, mint, $250.00 – 350.00.

Mickey Mouse cookie tin, 1930s, rare TV logo, $400.00 – 600.00.

Mickey Mouse Bavarian china pitcher, $200.00 – 300.00.

Mickey Mouse child's plate, by Salem China, 1930s, $125.00 – 200.00.

Mickey Mouse and Pluto Patriot China plate, 1930s, $150.00 – 225.00.

Mickey Mouse tea set in original box, Ohio Art, rare, $650.00 – 1,000.00.

Mickey and Minnie Mouse tin sand pail, Ohio Art, 1930s, $750.00 – 1,000.00.

Mickey and Minnie Mouse sand pail, 4", Ohio Art, mint with shovel, $750.00 – 950.00.

Mickey Mouse "Mickey's Garden" pail, Ohio Art, 1930s, $700.00 – 1,000.00.

Mickey Mouse fishing pail, Ohio Art, 1930s, rare, $2,200.00 – 3,500.00.

Mickey and Minnie Mouse gondoliers pail, Ohio Art, $1,500.00 – 2,000.00.

Mickey Mouse treasure island pail, Ohio Art, 1930s, $700.00 – 1,000.00.

Mickey Mouse and friends
giant 12" diameter toy top,
1930s, $500.00 – 750.00.

Left: Mickey and Minnie Mouse handcar,
by Lionel, 1930s, $600.00 – 900.00.
Right: Mickey Mouse wood composition
barker figure, 1930s, $200.00 – 350.00.

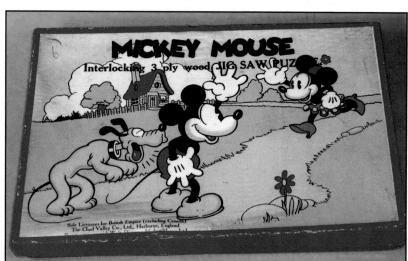

Mickey Mouse boxed puzzles set, by Chad Valley of England, $300.00 – 400.00.

Mickey Mouse drummer pull toy, by Fisher Price, 1930s,
$1,200.00 – 1,600.00.

Mickey Mouse sweeper, excellent tin lithography, $500.00 – 750.00.

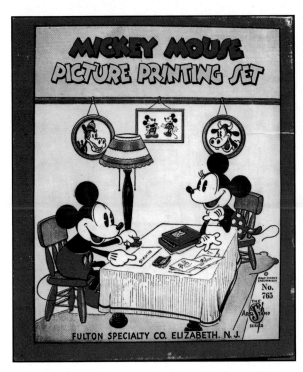

Mickey Mouse Picture Printing Set, by Fulton, 1930s, $275.00 – 400.00.

Mickey Mouse dominoes, by Halsam, 1930s, in original box, $275.00 – 400.00.

Mickey Mouse Soldier Set, by Marks Brothers of Boston, $550.00 – 900.00.

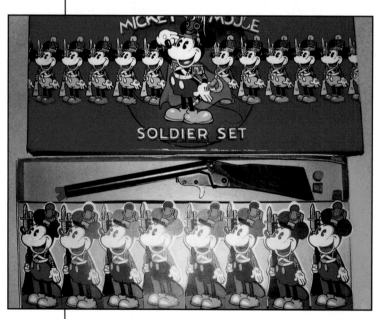

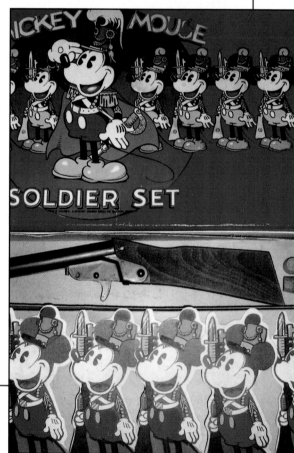

Mickey Mouse Safety Blocks, by Halsam, 1930s, $300.00 – 450.00.

Mickey and Minnie Mouse die-cut puzzle, wood, 1930s, $300.00 – 400.00.

Mickey Mouse The Three Pals bisque set in box, Japan, $900.00 – 1,400.00.

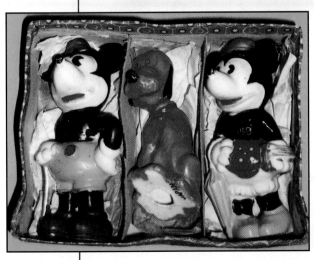

The Pop-Up Mickey Mouse, by Blue Ribbon Books, $550.00 – 800.00.

Donald Duck composition windup, 14" tall, 1930s, rare, $1,500.00 – 2,200.00.

Donald Duck jointed doll, wood composition, $1,700.00 – 2,200.00.

Donald Duck squeak toy, Seiberling Latex Products, 1930s, $250.00 – 350.00.

Donald Duck bisque figure, Japan, 1930s, 4" tall, $350.00 – 475.00.

Donald Duck celluloid jointed figure, 6" tall, Japan, $650.00 – 1,000.00.

Donald Duck pull toy, Fisher Price, 1930s, $700.00 – 900.00.

Long-billed Donald Duck Chick Cart, Fisher Price, rare, $900.00 – 1,200.00.

Donald Duck storybook, very colorful illustrations, 1930s, $300.00 – 450.00.

Donald Duck pot metal still bank,
rare, $500.00 – 750.00.

Long-billed Donald Duck planter, glazed
ceramic, rare, $500.00 – 700.00.

Double Donald Duck bisque toothbrush holder, $375.00 – 500.00.

Snow White celluloid figural doll,
6" tall, 1930s, $250.00 – 400.00.

Happy the Dwarf doll, by Richard
Krueger, 1937 , $450.00 – 700.00.

Disney's Happy Dwarf doll, 1930s,
$400.00 – 600.00.

Grumpy the Dwarf doll, 1930s
$400.00 – 600.00.

Disney's Sleepy Dwarf doll,
1930s, $400.00 – 600.00.

Bashful the Dwarf doll, 1930s,
$400.00 – 600.00.

Disney's Sneezy Dwarf doll,
1930s, $400.00 – 600.00.

Dopey composition bank,
by Crown Toy and Novelty,
$200.00 – 300.00.

Snow White tin sand pail, by Ohio
Art, 1937, $400.00 – 650.00.

Snow White and Dopey dime register banks, $200.00 – 250.00 each.

Dopey Dwarf pull toy, manufactured by Fisher Price,
1938, $600.00 – 900.00.

Disney's Snow White and the Dwarfs boxed set, Seiberling, $1,500.00 – 2,000.00.

Snow White and the Dwarfs pull toy, by N. N. Hill Brass, $900.00 – 1,200.00.

Pinocchio jointed doll, wood composition, by Crown Toy, $350.00 – 500.00.

Pinocchio doll, by Ideal Toy and Novelty, 12", $650.00 – 1,000.00.

Pinocchio doll, by Knickerbocker, 10", ca. 1939, $500.00 – 800.00.

Pinocchio on turtle composition bank, by Crown, rare, $700.00 – 900.00.

Pinocchio doll, in original box, by Ideal, 1940, $550.00 – 750.00.

Pinocchio bank, by Crown Toy and Novelty, 1939, $350.00 – 475.00.

Pinocchio Race Game, by Chad Valley of England, $200.00 – 350.00.

Jiminy Cricket doll, by Ideal Toy and Novelty, $600.00 – 900.00.

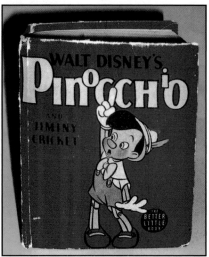

Walt Disney's Pinocchio and Jiminy Cricket Better Little Book, by Whitman, $75.00 – 110.00.

Pinocchio Puppet Show, by Whitman, ca. 1939, $350.00 – 500.00.

Pinocchio Express, by Fisher Price, 1939, $800.00 – 1,200.00.

Thread spool animals, paper lithographed, $75.00 – 100.00.

Horse figure, celluloid, 5" long, $40.00 – 80.00.

Standing horse, celluloid, 5" long, $35.00 – 65.00.

Walking dog celluloid figure, excellent paint, $75.00 – 125.00.

Camel, celluloid, 4" long, $35.00 – 65.00.

Cow push toy, paper composition, 1930s, $125.00 – 250.00.

Buffalo celluloid figure, 6" long, $50.00 – 75.00.

Running Scottie dog, in original box, Louis Marx, $400.00 – 600.00.

Tall bunny figure with glass eyes, paper composition, $200.00 – 300.00.

Lion figure, celluloid, 4" long, $40.00 – 75.00.

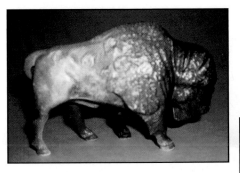

Buffalo figural celluloid toy, 4" long, $35.00 – 65.00.

Ram figure, celluloid, 5" long, $35.00 – 65.00.

Floating fish, bright colors, celluloid, $40.00 – 75.00.

Duck, brightly colored, celluloid, 4" long, $35.00 – 65.00.

Duck figure, celluloid, 4" long, $35.00 – 65.00.

Floating swan, celluloid, $50.00 – 100.00.

Chicken and egg cart, tin lithographed, $200.00 – 325.00.

Froggy the Gremlin squeak toy, by
Rempel Toys, $125.00 – 150.00.

Scrappy pull toy, extremely rare, $750.00 – 1,000.00.

Betty Boop ukelele, with Koko and
Bimbo, rare, $250.00 – 400.00.

Bunny and chick cart, tin lithographed, $200.00 – 300.00.

Chein tin toy top, 1930s, $100.00 – 200.00.

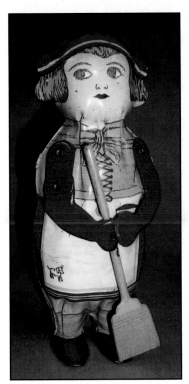

Lindstrom windup maid tin lithographed action toy, $300.00 – 450.00.

Lindstrom Mammy Maid tin lithographed action toy, $400.00 – 600.00.

Kiddie Cyclist incredible realistic action toy, by Unique Art, $700.00 – 1,000.00.

Courtland red dump truck, "A Walt Reach Toy," in box, $400.00 – 600.00.

Zilotone musical disc toy, by Wolverine, $400.00 – 700.00.

Buck Rogers Space Ranger punch-out set, premium, $250.00 – 400.00.

Buttercup and Spare Ribs pull toy, rare, $1,000.00 – 1,500.00.

Cartoon Character box of Christmas light bulbs, $150.00 – 200.00.

Dick Tracy and Sparkle Plenty Christmas Tree Lights set, $200.00 – 300.00.

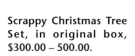

Scrappy Christmas Tree Set, in original box, $300.00 – 500.00.

Baby Boomers know full well that they are a rare breed. No other generation followed such a great war as World War II, and no other generation was as immediately doted on and rewarded with the fruition of the hopes and dreams of their parents. When the war was over, a virtual demographic onslaught of babies, then youngsters, hit the sidewalks of American suburbia. And the world of toy production and the toy industry itself would never be the same.

This is the era of hula hoops and Disneyland, color television and *Bonanza*, Saturday matinees and after school cartoons, *Leave it to Beaver* and *Ozzie and Harriet*. Toys in the 1950s and 1960s were more media inspired than ever before, and this time it was all about the electronic media. Two decades earlier, children found their heroes in the comic strip pages, on the radio, or at the movies. Now, in the 1950s and 1960s, the popular medium was television, and toy manufacturers immediately understood the marketing power of the picture tube. Companies like Mattel and Remco advertised heavily, especially in the midst of Saturday morning cartoons and after school time slots. Since cable television wasn't to be heard of for another 20 or 30 years, the children of these two decades had a choice of maybe three channels to watch, and advertisers zeroed in on the boomers who watched glued to televisions with tiny black and white picture tubes. As the televisions evolved, so did the commercials to the point that it was quite easy for a good jingle to create an overnight fad, one that would engulf millions of children and send them bounding to the dime stores that next weekend. Remco was the master of the toy jingle. Their clever lyrics and singable tunes became household hits, bordering on folk music. Once a kid got a jingle in his or her head, they couldn't stop thinking about the toy. Consider Remco's mid-1960s creation, Mr. Kelly's Car Wash (a mint in the box example of this popular toy is pictured in this chapter). The car wash jingle went something like "Mister Kelly's Car Wash, that's the toy for me!" and then the lyrics proceeded to tell you all that the toy did, and why you just had to have one. This particular toy has a great personal significance for me. In 1964,

Rabbit, tin windup, Japan, holding a carrot with cloth leaves, $125.00 – 200.00.

I was in the fifth grade and still a believer in Santa — I mean really a believer. I had no doubt that the jolly old elf actually lived at the North Pole and was flesh and blood. Oh, there were scoffers in my neighborhood, but until the Christmas morning packages went away or somebody could prove it to me otherwise, Santa was, and always had been, real. Well, starting in October of 1964 when the jingle first hit the Saturday morning cartoons, I learned the song. And there was no question that I was going to own a Mr. Kelly's Car Wash, even if it was to be the only toy Santa would bring me that year. In '64, I was already 10 years old, and one of those latch key kids so pitied in recent years. We lived on a small mini-farm, so when I got off the school bus, it was just me heading into the house. I had heard enough about moms and dads and their links with Santa, and I was fed up. Something in the waning recesses of my childhood prompted me to search the house. It was barely a week after Thanksgiving, and about 10 minutes into the search, I found it! A perfectly wonderful Remco's Mr. Kelly's Car Wash in its brightly colored elongated box was resting in the darkness under my mom and dad's bed. Either Santa had delivered it very early to save on express shipping charges, or my parents really did have a hand in helping Santa. So, with the help of this great toy, I learned a little more about the reality of Christmas than I really wanted to. But, in retrospect, knowing that the pristine toy was waiting for me in my parent's bedroom only made the anticipation grander. Every day when I got home from school (two hours before Mom got home and four hours before my Father) I would lie on my back, lift up the bed skirt and look beneath it. This became a daily ritual, and by the time Santa delivered it on Christmas morning, I tore into the box that had been sealed for way too long. And it was worth the wait, complete with a water tower that you could fill with real water, tiny cans of wax that would really wax the car, towels, sponges, and a motorized chain drive that pulled the cars through the car wash itself. This was an example of toy design perfection.

Other significant toy manufacturers of this period, in addition to Remco, were Hasbro and Mattel. Mattel Toys in particular struck a toy gold mine when they released their line of Western toy guns and play sets known as the Shootin Shell series. Prior to the late 1950s appearance (1958 – 1959) of guns that fired real plastic bullets, the predecessors of the Mattel guns series were Fanner 50 models. These "fanners" were named for the versatile ability of the young gunslinger to whip the palm of his hand across the top of the gun hammer in rapid action causing the cylinder to spin and shoot without ever actually pulling the trigger. The early "fanners" accepted real looking bullets attached permanently to metal shell casings. These were non-firing, but they looked like real bullets and could be loaded and removed just like real cartridges. Mattel struck marketing genius when they perfected on the decades old idea of the roll of caps being replaced by their own brand of Greenie Stickem Caps which could be affixed right onto the back of the cartridge casings and made the fake bullets have the sound of actually firing.

The later Shootin Shell models opened up the barrels so that a projectile could actually fly out of it. The bullet and cartridge became two separate pieces which had to be spring loaded. When the hammer hit the back of the cartridge loaded into the barrel of a rifle or a revolver, the hard plastic bullet head actually fired. These realistic firing toys wouldn't last very long in today's world filled with toy safety lawsuits and government warnings, but in 1959 when they first appeared… it was just plain cool Western toy fun! Who knows how many little brothers and sisters actually sustained eye injuries from these realistic guns? I would venture to say that the numbers had to be in the thousands… the temptation to actually shoot someone with these apparently harmless bullets was an urge that just had to be satisfied by the young sure-shot gunslinger. The examples shown in this chapter are near mint unused examples. Note the wonderful box art on the Shootin Shell Winchester rifle set complete with all caps and the cloth pouch of bullets and cartridges, the rare genuine leather Shootin Shell Fanner 50 set in its brand new box complete with instructions, cap boxes and bullet packs, and the outstanding mint example of Mattel's detective toy masterpiece, the Shootin Shell Snub Nose .38 which could make any youngster an instant F.B.I. man. Mattel boxed gun sets from the 1950s and 1960s are one of the hottest areas of collecting today…near mint

Colorful lithographed bird, tin windup,
$125.00 – 175.00.

and unused sets can bring prices in the high hundreds and even top $1,000 if the set is unusual and complete with instructions.

Another example of Mattel's fascination in the 1960s with the television detective trend was its Lie Detector game. Although the game required no batteries, it used a spring-loaded "pen" mechanism which gave clues on a meter readout by actually "reading" a secret punch card template that was concealed inside. This template could be changed or rotated from one game to the next, and both the box graphics and the suspect cards have a bizarre comic book style that to this day are both stunning and haunting. Mint condition sets of this much used, popular game are hard to find today. Since the Western was a 1950s staple of family time television entertainment, wonderful toys were manufactured in the likeness of the popular television heroes and stars. One major manufacturer of Western toys was The Hartland Plastics Company. This company manufactured wonderful cowboy heroes and their horses during the late 1950s and on into the 1960s. Even the original boxes were gorgeous with beautiful western graphics on all sides. Great examples of such characters as The Lone Ranger, Tonto, Wyatt Earp, Cheyenne, Matt Dillon from *Gunsmoke*, and Paladin from *Have Gun Will Travel* are just a few of the fun plastic heroes pictured in the chapter and manufactured by Hartland. Several famous New York Yankees players such as Babe Ruth, Mickey Mantle, Roger Maris, and Yogi Berra are also Hartland figures featured in this chapter.

Yet another phenomenon peculiar to the 1960s was the gas station premium toy. Texaco was famous for wonderful "fill up" promotions where an eight gallon purchase allowed a dad (or mom) to purchase a great Texaco brand toy. This chapter features the Texaco fire truck by Buddy L. in its original box, the Texaco fire chief hat in its original Texaco box and complete with working battery operated microphone, and a great old 1960s battery operated Texaco tanker ship. All of these sold in the three dollar to four dollar range which meant that a parent would pay about twice as much as a fill up on gas to purchase the toy (with gas at .25 cents per gallon, you could fill up with 12 gallons for $3.00, and the premium toys would then double the cost of your purchase). It was indeed a generous parent who would spring for a $3.00 toy at a gas station in the 1960s.

The space race brought wonderful science and space travel inspired toys during this period, and such television programs as *The Jetsons* and *Lost in Space* inspired fun toys. One of the unique things about these two decades in American history, aside from the fact that they represent the childhood and adolescence of the baby boomer generation, is the fact that the interests, passions, and goals of the era are reflected in the toys. Space age? It's represented in the toys of the 1950s and 1960s. Western Americana was evidenced through the popular television shows and movies of these two decades. You'll find it in the myriad of toys produced for both mail order catalogs and dime store sales. Being a child of the 1950s, I recognize a fondness for that period and an unavoidable bias toward the popular toys of Remco, Mattel, Ideal, and Hartland among others. There will never be such an explosion of growth, imagination, adventure, history, and pure fun as was offered up to the baby boomer generation in the 1950s and 1960s. The toys are classics from a unique two decades in our life stories. For novice collectors just beginning their collections or old timers like myself, when it comes to fun toys, no era beats the 1950s and 1960s.

Twin ducks in basket windup, $75.00 – 100.00.

Red bird tin windup, jumping action, $100.00 – 150.00.

Plastic dog on skiis windup, $50.00 – 75.00.

Furry squirrel windup, jumping action, $125.00 – 175.00.

Egg laying hen action toy, by Baldwin Mfg. Corp., $250.00 – 350.00.

Cat push puppet, wood and plastic, by Kohner, $75.00 – 100.00.

Dog jumping rope, tin windup, $125.00 – 200.00.

Bugs Bunny plastic character still bank, $50.00 – 75.00.

Steiff tiger, 10" long, no button in ear, 1960s, $75.00 – 125.00.

Lassie stuffed animal with plastic facial features, glass eyes, 1950s, $100.00 – 125.00.

Sinclair plastic dinosaur bank, 1960s, premium, $75.00 – 100.00.

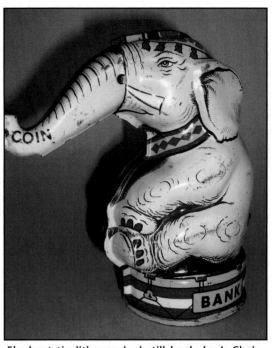

Elephant tin lithographed still bank, by J. Chein, $125.00 – 200.00.

Li'l Abner Can O' Coins still bank, 1960s, $45.00 – 75.00.

Plastic rocket toy, launches top, by Multiple Plastics, $125.00 – 200.00.

Cast metal outer space mechanical bank, 1950s, $200.00 – 300.00.

Captain Video Rocket Launcher set, in original box, 1950s, $200.00 – 300.00.

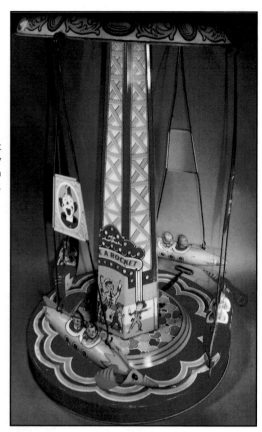

Ride a Rocket tin windup, by J. Chein, action lithographed toy, $450.00 – 600.00.

Lost in Space Game, by Milton Bradley, 1966, rare, $300.00 – 500.00.

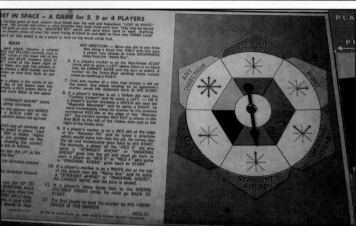

Lost in Space photo autographed by Angela Cartwright, $150.00 – 250.00.

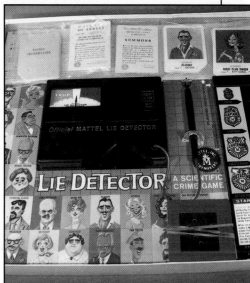

Mattel Lie Detector game, "Scientific Crime Game," 1960s, $150.00 – 250.00.

Kentucky Derby Racing Game, Whitman, 1960s, $50.00 – 75.00.

The Jetsons Game,
Hanna Barbera,
Milton Bradley
Games, 1960s,
$200.00 – 300.00.

The Jetsons Jigsaw Puzzle, published
by Whitman, $75.00 – 100.00.

Superman Paint by Numbers,
rare set, $250.00 – 375.00.

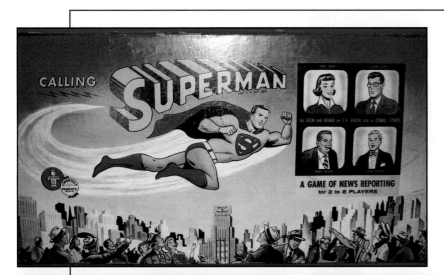

Calling Superman board game, by Transogram, rare, circa 1954, $350.00 – 500.00.

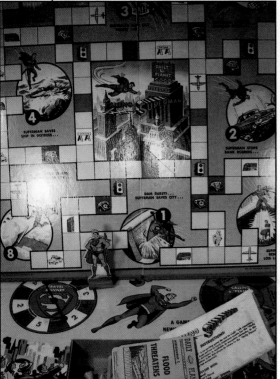

Casper the Friendly Ghost board game, by Milton Bradley, $125.00 – 175.00.

Tinkertoys building play set, all wooden, in bright canister, 1960s, $75.00 – 125.00.

Felix the Cat Target Set, in box with four darts, $150.00 – 250.00.

Dale Evans and Buttermilk, $25.00 – 50.00.

Wagon Train T.V. series book, 1950s, $65.00 – 90.00.

Rin Tin Tin and the Ghost Wagon Train, 1950s, $45.00 – 65.00.

Warner Brothers *Cheyenne and the Lost Gold*, $45.00 – 75.00.

Rin Tin Tin coloring book, 1950s, $55.00 – 95.00.

Have Gun Will Travel, Paladin storybook, CBS, $75.00 – 100.00.

Maverick T.V. series book, copyright Warner Brothers, $50.00 – 75.00.

Walt Disney's Tonka, a hardcover book, 1950s, $55.00 – 75.00.

Bat Masterson T.V. series book, Whitman, 1950s, $75.00 – 100.00.

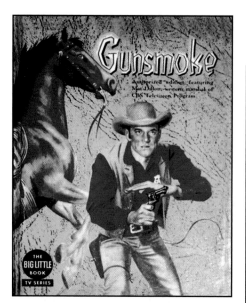

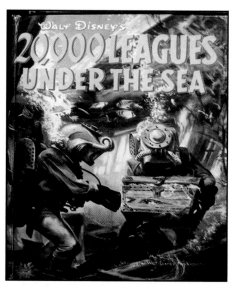

Gunsmoke T.V. series, Big Little Book, by Whitman, $75.00 – 100.00.

Voyage to the Bottom of the Sea, $35.00 – 50.00.

Walt Disney's 20,000 Leagues Under the Sea, Whitman, $50.00 – 75.00.

Beautiful Joe, 1960s, $20.00 – 30.00.

Lassie and the Secret of the Summer, Whitman T.V. book, $50.00 – 75.00.

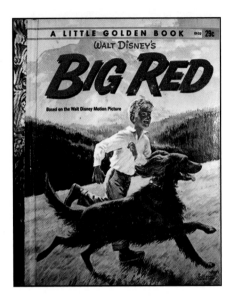

Walt Disney's Big Red, Little Golden Book, $20.00 – 30.00.

Lassie, The Forbidden Valley, T.V. book, $50.00 – 75.00.

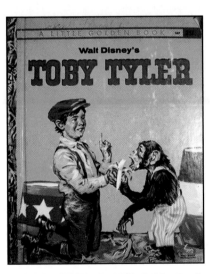

Walt Disney's Toby Tyler, Little Golden Book, $20.00 – 30.00.

Dondi, Wonder Books, $25.00 – 45.00.

The Walton Boys in Rapids Ahead, Whitman Boy's Book, $25.00 – 35.00.

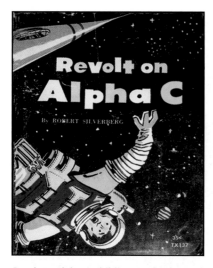

Revolt on Alpha C, child's paperback novel, 1960s, $10.00 – 15.00.

Golden Library of Knowledge, three space books 1960s, $75.00 – 125.00.

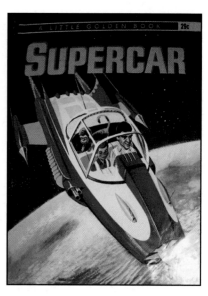

Supercar, Little Golden Book, 1960s, $25.00 – 55.00.

Huckleberry Hound, Big Golden Book, 1960s, $35.00 – 55.00.

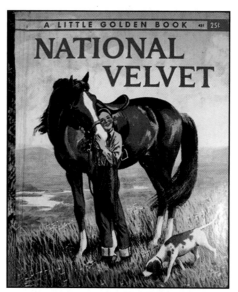

National Velvet, Little Golden Book, 1950s, $20.00 – 30.00.

Circus Time, Little Golden activity book, moving cover disc, rare, $35.00 – 50.00.

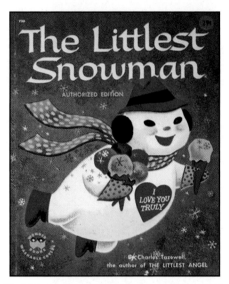

The Littlest Snowman, Wonder Books, $20.00 – 30.00.

The Happiest Christmas, 1950s, $15.00 – 25.00.

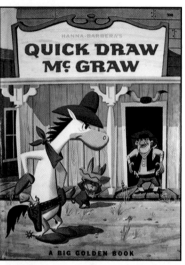

Quick Draw McGraw, Big Golden Book, 1960s, $35.00 – 55.00.

The Mouseketeers Tryout Time, Whitman, Tell-A-Tale Books, $30.00 – 50.00.

Leave it to Beaver, Whitman, T.V. Series books, $50.00 – 70.00.

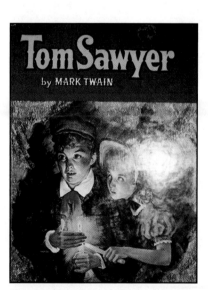

Tom Sawyer, by Mark Twain, Whitman book, 1960s, $20.00 – 30.00.

Hopalong Cassidy lunch box, Alladin Industries, 1950s, $300.00 – 400.00 set.

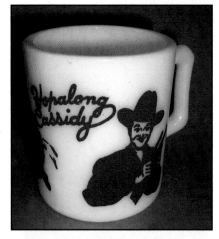

Hopalong Cassidy milk glass mug, 1950s, $45.00 – 80.00.

Hopalong Cassidy cap pistol, 1950s, $135.00 – 200.00.

Hopalong Cassidy Bar 20 ranch motion light, rare, $300.00 – 500.00.

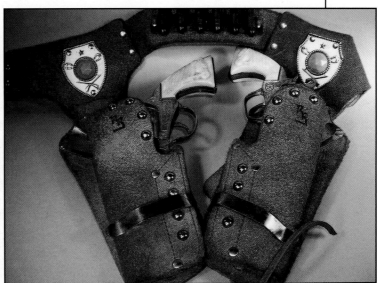

Roy Rogers Flash Draw Holster Outfit, in original box, $400.00 – 700.00.

Roy Rogers plastic cup, excellent condition, $50.00 – 75.00.

Roy Rogers on Trigger (rearing), Hartland Plastics figure, $200.00 – 325.00.

Roy Rogers Ranch Lantern, in box, Ohio Art Co., $250.00 – 350.00.

Lone Ranger on Silver, Hartland Plastics, original, $200.00 – 325.00.

Tonto from The Lone Ranger, Hartland Plastics, $200.00 – 300.00.

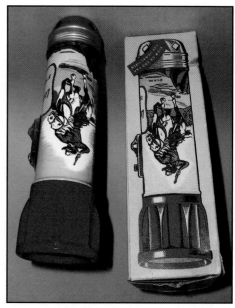

Lone Ranger flashlight, in original box, $250.00 – 350.00.

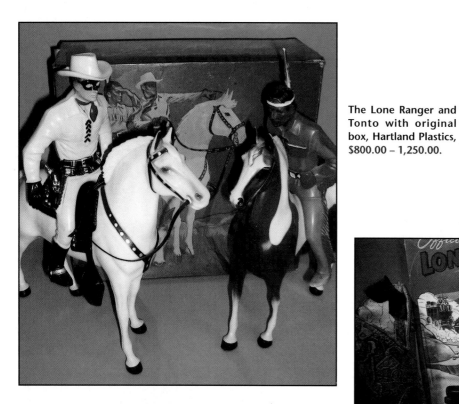

The Lone Ranger and Tonto with original box, Hartland Plastics, $800.00 – 1,250.00.

Official Lone Ranger boots, by Endicott-Johnson, in box, $500.00 – 750.00.

Zorro ceramic pencil holder and sharpener, Enesco, $100.00 – 150.00.

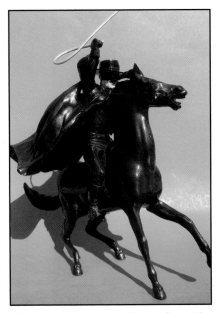

Walt Disney's Zorro and horse, by Louis Marx, 10" long, $150.00 – 225.00.

Walt Disney's Zorro hand puppet, by Gund, 1950s, $75.00 – 125.00.

Walt Disney's *Zorro* authorized T.V. book, Whitman, $75.00 – 125.00.

Walt Disney's *The Adventures of Zorro*, Big Golden Book, $75.00 – 100.00.

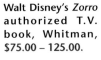

Zorro wrist watch in original box, 1950s, rare, $300.00 – 450.00.

Walt Disney's Mickey Mouse Club, Zorro record, 1950s, $50.00 – 75.00.

Bonanza lunch box and thermos set, original, $200.00 – 350.00.

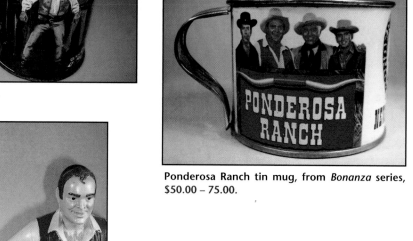

Ponderosa Ranch tin mug, from *Bonanza* series, $50.00 – 75.00.

Bonanza, professionally built up model display, rare, $250.00 – 400.00.

Cochise on horse, by Hartland Plastics, all original, $125.00 – 200.00.

Seth Adams/Ward Bond from *Wagon Train* Hartland Plastics, $250.00 – 350.00.

Cheyenne, with horse and gun, Hartland Plastics, $275.00 – 375.00.

Wyatt Earp, with horse, saddle, reins, and hat, Hartland Plastics, $200.00 – 300.00.

Paladin from *Have Gun Will Travel*, Hartland Plastics, $300.00 – 400.00.

Sheriff Matt Dillon from *Gunsmoke*, Hartland Plastics, $250.00 – 350.00.

Chief Thunderbird on horseback, Hartland Plastics, $200.00 – 325.00.

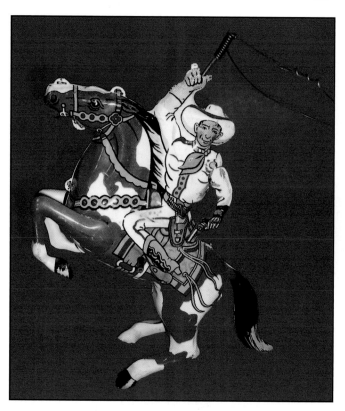

Cowboy on horse tin windup, near mint, $350.00 – 550.00.

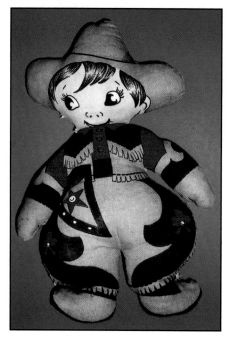

Cowboy rag doll, stuffed cotton fabric, 1960, $50.00 – 75.00.

Gene Autry rubber cowboy boots, ca. 1950s, $150.00 – 225.00.

Buffalo Bill Jr. western belt on display card, $45.00 – 75.00.

Wagon and two horses, Auburn Rubber, 1950s, $50.00 – 75.00.

Davy Crockett and two horses, rubber, $35.00 – 65.00.

Cowboys and Indians, rubber, three pieces, $30.00 – 50.00.

Cowboys and Indians, rubber, three pieces, $30.00 – 50.00.

Indians, rubber, set of five pieces, 1950s, $30.00 – 65.00.

Model Shooting Gallery windup, by Wyandotte, $200.00 – 350.00.

Mattel Shootin' Shell Fanner 50, double holster set, $600.00 – 1,000.00.

Mattel Shootin' Shell Winchester Rifle set, in original box, $400.00 – 750.00.

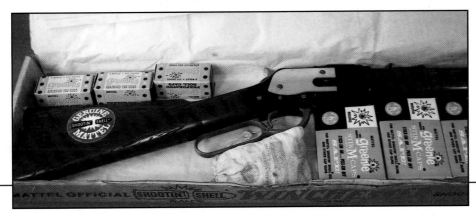

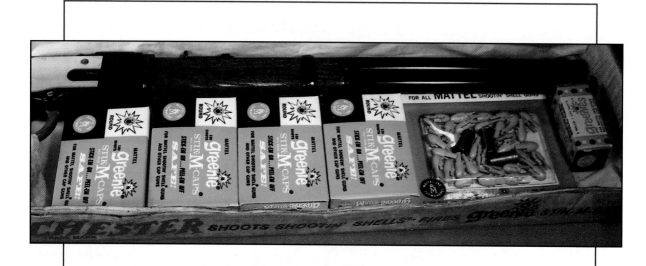

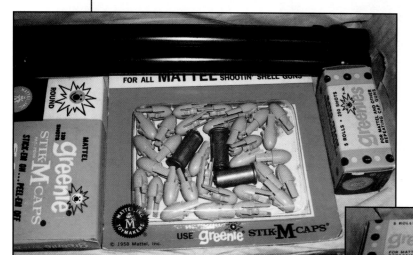

Mattel Shootin' Shell Winchester Rifle set, in original box, $400.00 – 750.00.

Mattel Bullet-Loading Fanner 50 gun set in original box, $350.00 – 500.00.

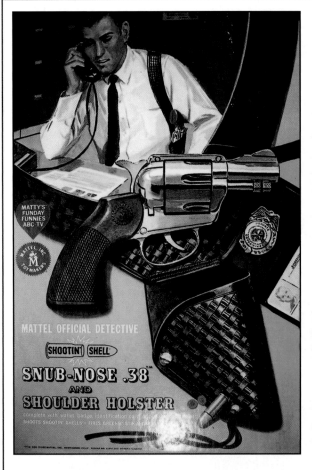

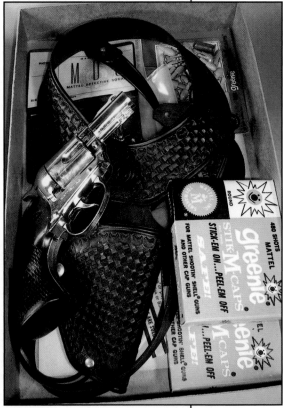

Mattel Shootin' Shell
Snub Nose .38 and
Shoulder Holster,
in original box,
$450.00 – 750.00.

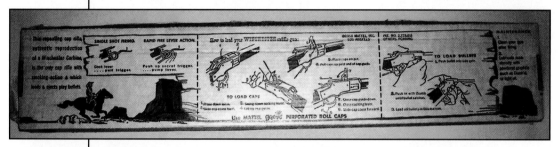

Mattel Official Winchester Saddle Gun, in original box, $400.00 – 700.00.

Kit Carson cap gun, fires caps, excellent condition, $95.00 – 145.00.

Gene Autry cap pistol, metal, 1950s, $135.00 – 225.00.

Rex Mars Planet Patrol Sparkling Pistol, by Louis Marx, in box, $200.00 – 350.00.

Dragnet Detective Special Revolver, in original box, $350.00 – 475.00.

Dragnet Crime Lab play set, Jack Webb on box lid, rare, $350.00 – 450.00.

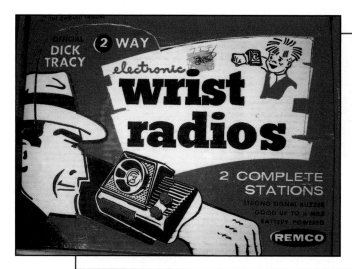

Dick Tracy Two Way Wrist Radios, by Remco, in box, outer box and inside contents shown. $250.00 – 350.00.

Dick Tracy Sub-Machine Water Gun, in original box, $250.00 – 375.00.

Dick Tracy squad car, battery operated, tin lithograph, $300.00 – 400.00.

Dick Tracy boy's set, with suspenders, badge, etc. in box, $200.00 – 300.00.

Shell Premium rocket car, by WEN-MAC, AMC, $350.00 – 450.00.

Race car, 12" long with rolling wheels, by Auburn Rubber, $125.00 – 200.00.

Roadsters, by Processed Plastics, 1960s, $65.00 – 135.00 pair.

Roadsters, by Processed Plastics, 1960s, $65.00 – 135.00 pair.

Giant Roadster by Processed Plastics, 10" long, 1960s, $125.00 – 200.00.

Yellow roadster, by Processed Plastics, 1960s, $25.00 – 55.00.

Corvette, by Korris Kars 1960s, $50.00 – 100.00.

Ford Thunderbird, by Korris Kars, 1960s, $45.00 – 75.00.

Policeman on motorcycle, by Auburn Rubber, 1950s, $50.00 – 75.00.

Mustang plastic car, 12" long, probably by Korris Kars, $75.00 – 125.00.

Mr. Magoo tin lithographed old time character car, vinyl head, $400.00 – 750.00.

Plastic rodeo cowboy Jeep windup and tin toy, $250.00 – 300.00.

Tootsietoy boxed Jeep and howitzer, $150.00 – 250.00.

Red dump truck, cranking bed, by Smith Miller (Smitty), $350.00 – 500.00.

Metal Masters red pickup truck, $125.00 – 200.00.

Pickup truck, silver colored bed, by Tootsietoy, $65.00 – 100.00.

Cement mixer with cranking mixer tank, by Tootsietoy, $75.00 – 150.00.

Milk and ice cream truck, plastic, friction drive, advertising tie-in, $75.00 – 125.00.

Red fire truck, all rubber, by Auburn Rubber, 1950s, $75.00 – 100.00.

Friction fire truck with working ladder, Japan, 1960s, $120.00 – 175.00.

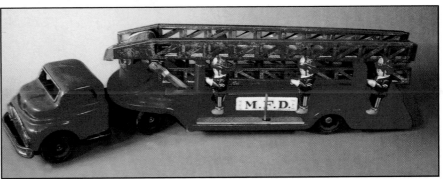

Texaco fire chief truck, by Buddy L,
with original box, $750.00 – 950.00.

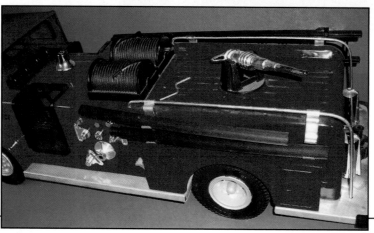

Texaco fire chief hat, gas premium with box, 1960s, $250.00 – 400.00.

Battery operated Texaco toy tanker, 1960s gasoline premium, $250.00 – 500.00.

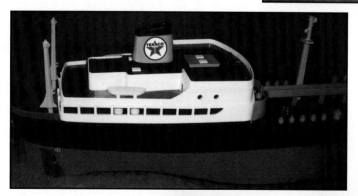

Tonka fire chief truck, 1960s, $350.00 – 500.00.

Tonka Serv-i-Car, steers and bed empties, rare, 1960s, $200.00 – 300.00.

Tonka Service delivery truck, blue, with ladder, $250.00 – 375.00.

Tonka farm truck, with original animals, trailer, and box, $500.00 – 750.00.

Tonka Marine Service truck, with custom decals, a trailer, and boats, $375.00 – 600.00.

Tonka tan pickup truck, box, and catalog, $400.00 – 700.00.

Tonka tan pickup catalog.

Green friction tractor with cart, made in Japan, $200.00 – 300.00.

Green farm tractor, 5" long, by Auburn Rubber, $75.00 – 100.00.

Red farm tractor, 4" long, by Auburn Rubber, $75.00 – 100.00.

WWII style airplane, by Hubley, $150.00 – 200.00.

Diecast twin prop plane, moving propellers, mint, $150.00 – 250.00.

Hubley yellow and green plane with plastic cockpit, $175.00 – 275.00.

Hubley Navy fighter plane, in original box, $250.00 – 350.00.

Hubley red and yellow plane, missing cockpit, $125.00 – 150.00.

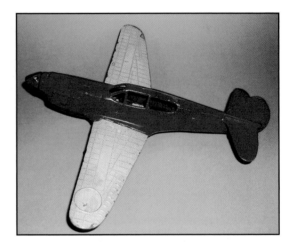

Hubley diecast plane, $75.00 – 125.00.

Sea plane, floating action windup tin toy, by J. Chein, $200.00 – 300.00.

Remote control helicopter tin windup, West Germany, $250.00 – 350.00.

Submarine tin windup toy, floats, by Wolverine, $250.00 – 350.00.

Plastic submarine with firing torpedoes, by Ideal Toy, $75.00 – 125.00.

U.S. Destroyer
with original box,
by Ideal Toys,
$250.00 – 350.00.

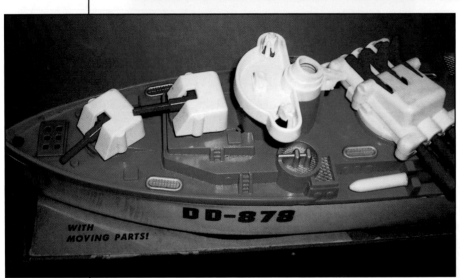

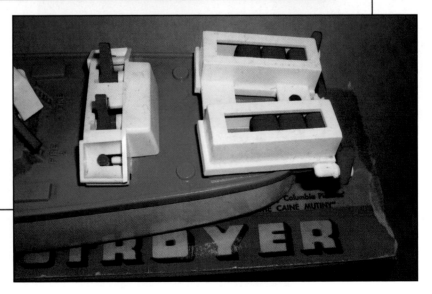

Batman Picture Pistol in original box, projects images, $250.00 – 350.00.

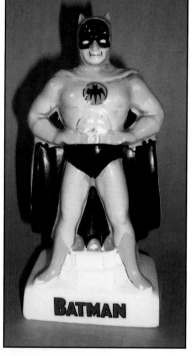

Batman ceramic bank, approximately 8" tall, $125.00 – 175.00.

Batman and Robin car with original dolls, 10" long, $150.00 – 275.00.

Batman and Robin bookends, original paint, $150.00 – 275.00.

Howdy Doody in spaceship bank, $75.00 – 100.00.

Howdy Doody Ovaltine plastic cup, 1950s, $50.00 – 75.00.

Howdy Doody tin windup band, Howdy and Bob Smith, $800.00 – 1,200.00.

Howdy Doody premium Ovaltine mug, ca. 1950s, $50.00 – 75.00.

Howdy Doody bubble bath in container, colorful box, $125.00 – 200.00.

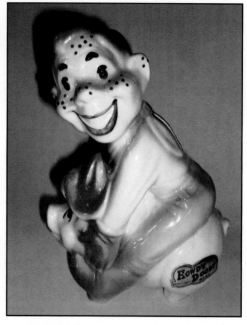

Howdy Doody ceramic bank, with original sticker, 1950s, $200.00 – 325.00.

Howdy Doody trapeze toy, tin, metal, plastic, and composition, $400.00 – 600.00.

Howdy Doody's Three Ring Circus, Wiry Dan electric game, $250.00 – 375.00.

Popeye spinach in the can, $20.00 – 30.00.

Popeye tin windup tank, lithographed tin, by Line Mar, Japan, $450.00 – 600.00.

Popeye and Sweet Pea pull toy, by Metal Masters, rare, $400.00 – 650.00.

Popeye jointed plastic doll, by Cameo, 14" tall, $250.00 – 350.00.

Fred Flintstone vinyl doll, 12" tall, $75.00 – 125.00.

Dino the Dinosaur vinyl doll, 13" tall, $65.00 – 120.00.

Barney Rubble vinyl doll, 10" tall, $75.00 – 125.00.

Fred Flintstone and Barney Rubble tin windup on Dino, by LineMar, Japan, $400.00 – 700.00 each.

Barney Rubble and Fred Flintstone plastic car, $75.00 – 100.00.

Pebbles and Bam Bam Flintstone plastic car, $75.00 – 100.00.

Snoopy the astronaut play figure, 10" tall with space-suit, $125.00 – 175.00.

Space patrol battery operated rocket with Snoopy astronaut, $300.00 – 450.00.

Peanuts musical bus, rare, $250.00 – 375.00.

Snoopy in the bathtub bubble crank toy, $50.00 – 65.00.

Peanuts Thermos, great lithography, 1960s, front and back views, $125.00 – 175.00.

Peanuts marching band drum, tin lithographed, 14", rare, $250.00 – 375.00.

Peanuts lunch box, lithographed, 1960s, $150.00 – 200.00.

Mickey Mouse Mousegetar Junior, in original box, by Mattel, $150.00 – 225.00.

Casper the Friendly Ghost music box, by Mattel, 1961, $135.00 – 175.00.

Flipper in the music box, tin lithograph by Mattel, 1960s, $200.00 – 300.00.

Clown jack in the box, tin lithograph and plastic, musical, $75.00 – 125.00.

Mr. Kelly's Car Wash, Remco, 1960s, battery operated, with box, $375.00 – 550.00.

Babe Ruth, Hartland Plastics Toy, all original, $150.00 – 275.00.

Yogi Berra, Hartland Plastics Toy, all original, $225.00 – 325.00.

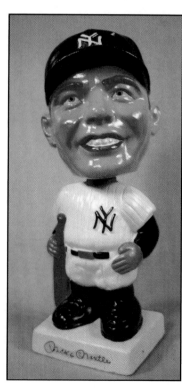

Mickey Mantle, Hartland Plastics Toy, all original, $250.00 – 350.00.

Roger Maris, Hartland Plastics Toy, all original, $200.00 – 300.00.

Mickey Mantle bobble head, mint condition, unusual, $350.00 – 500.00.

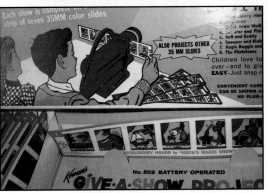

Kenner's Give a Show Projector with filmstrips, 1960s, $150.00 – 200.00.

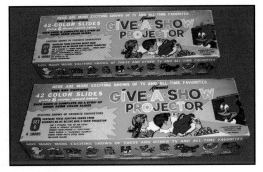

Kenner Give a Show Projector film boxes, 1960, $75.00 – 125.00 pair.

View-Master set, with eight original reel packets in box, 1960s, $125.00 – 200.00.

Terry and the Pirates picture records, $50.00 – 75.00.

Flash Gordon picture record, $75.00 – 125.00.

Flash Gordon City of Sea Caves picture record, $75.00 – 125.00.

Ball-bouncing girl tin and plastic windup, action, $200.00 – 300.00.

Santa Claus windup action, $125.00 – 200.00.

Charlie Weaver bartender battery operated windup toy, $250.00 – 375.00.

Rocky and Bullwinkle Soaky toys, by Colgate, 1960s, $75.00 – 125.00 pair.

Louis Armstrong windup figure, great action, $200.00 – 350.00.

Porky Pig tin windup cowboy toy, tin and plastic, $350.00 – 600.00.

Baba Louie, Hanna Barbera plush toy, ca. 1960, $150.00 – 225.00.

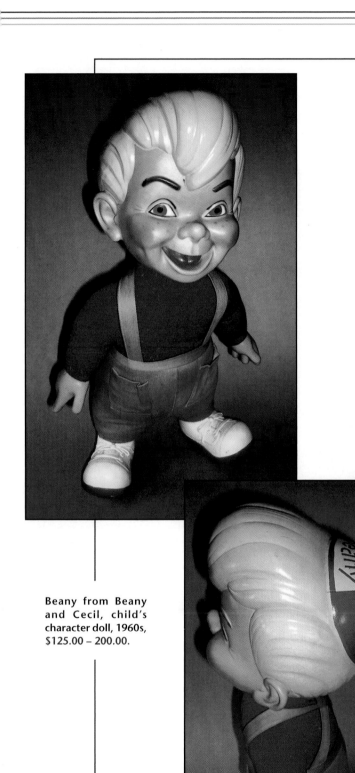

Beany from Beany and Cecil, child's character doll, 1960s, $125.00 – 200.00.

Big Boy vinyl squeak toy, 1960s, $25.00 – 35.00.

Li'l Abner and Daisy Mae chalk figures, 1950s, $125.00 – 175.00 set.

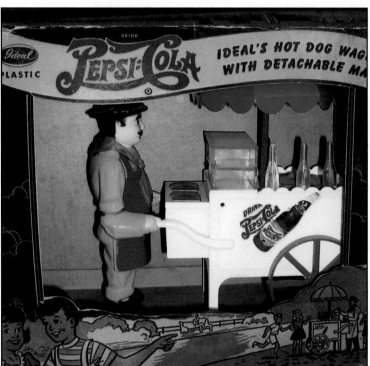

Pepsi Cola hot dog vendor, in original box, by Ideal, $200.00 – 300.00.

J. Fred Muggs pull toy, NBC News monkey, 1950s, $225.00 – 350.00.

Donald Duck mechanical whirling tail tin windup, LineMar Toys, $450.00 – 600.00.

Walt Disney's Donald and Pluto rocking chair, tin and celluloid, $600.00 – 900.00.

Ferris wheel windup, by
J. Chein, Hercules model,
$350.00 – 450.00.

Playland Merry Go Round
tin windup action toy, 14",
1950s, $350.00 – 500.00.

Yoyo, Mardi Gras by Duncan, Disney's Wonderful World of Color, $75.00 – 125.00.

Yoyo, multicolor plastic, Mardi Gras by Duncan, 1960s, $65.00 – 110.00.

Child's football helmet, Sears Roebuck, 1960s, $50.00 – 75.00.

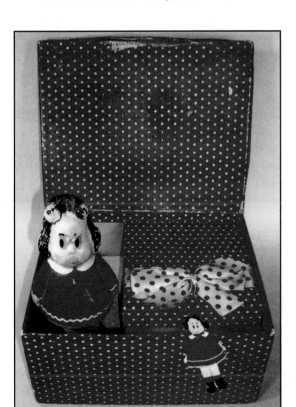

Little Lulu toiletries in the box, 1950s, rare set, $200.00 – 300.00.

Flash Gordon three puzzle set, by Milton Bradley, in original box, $200.00 – 325.00.

Modern Toys

The most important chapter in any toy price guide may indeed be the chapter devoted to today's collectibles. Our brief sample of toys pictured from the 1980s, 1990s, and onward into the new millennium is quite small because the sample is just a tiny representative one. The toys pictured here by no means represent all of the varied interests of mass toy production during the last 30 years. What they do represent is the fact that color, clever design, and unique new characters continue to appear on the market even to the present day.

The 1970s saw the advent of toys inspired by the Smurfs, Strawberry Shortcake, Scooby Doo, and new Hanna Barbera characters and the beginning popularity of toys inspired by Jim Henson's *Sesame Street*. The 1980s saw the birth of the Care Bears, *Fraggle Rock* (on Cable TV), and the beginnings of cable television inspired toys. The 1990s brought Furbies, Nickelodeon Network inspired spin-off toys, and the never to be forgotten Beanie Babies. I was caught up in the Beanie Baby craze because my own daughter was the prime demographic when they first emerged… under six, crazy about stuffed animals, and totally devoted to collecting them. As a father, I remember driving from one McDonald's restaurant to another in the passionate search for the week's latest release of mini-Beanie Babies offered with Happy Meals. Why did I do it? Because it made my daughter happy and she was, at the time, consumed with Beanie Baby mania. We bought dozens of them, and even went after the rare (if you can call any toy only six years earlier rare) ones that fetched a premium price. We stood in lines at Hallmark stores, we went to Beanie swap meets, we read magazines devoted to Beanie Baby collecting. Looking back, I remember my daughter's childhood as wonderful, but the whole Beanie Baby thing was just weird. At one point in the phenomenon (and I am certain, to my publisher's relief now) I considered trying to write the ultimate Beanie Baby price guide with projections on how Beanie Babies were here to stay and that

Ty Beanie Baby, with original hang tag, from 2000, $15.00 – 25.00.

if you played your Beanie Baby cards right, you might just be able to pay your kid's way through college by investing in the right, rare Beanie Babies. Just about the time that I was considering proposing this new book, Ty Warner, the founder of the whole Beanie Baby industry pulled the plug out of the Beanie Baby fortune bathwater, he ended the old line of Beanie Babies, put a halt to current production, vowed that they would not be subject to future distribution problems and scarcity, and even re-released new named version of older rare models. Beanie Baby collecting continued, but the greed was halted. It was a smart move by Mr. Warner. He wasn't interested in the secondary market of his little creations, he was interested only in the sales of the new ones. The secondary market craze and super fad was making it hard for normal people to just buy Beanie Babies for the sheer fun of it. By pretty much controlling distribution and ensuring ample supplies of all new releases, Ty virtually ended the profiteering of secondary market Beanie Baby dealers. And by doing so, he insured that his fun line of toys would outlast the fads, which it did.

So, the 1990s brought us Beanie Babies. The new millennium has seen rapid growth; and interest in high-tech toys, particularly those driven by sophisticated software which virtually stores enough memory to make toys act alive. One such example was the T.M.X. Tickle Me Elmo manufactured by Fisher Price in the fall of 2006. If there was ever a "toy of the year" that should be celebrated in a price guide, it was that one. The toy was in tremendously short supply around Christmas of 2006, and it didn't start reaching the toy shelves in plentiful supply until the spring of 2007. Although T.M.X. Tickle Me Elmo could be regarded as a fad toy, it is, in truth, much more. It represents a whole new genre of toys which will be appearing in our vastly expanding microcomputer chip age. The little Sesame Street character not only features a wonderful progressive vocabulary as you tickle him in an interactive way, he eventually works himself up into hysterics. I have seen toddlers flat out belly laugh when they watch him, and everyone of my three golden retrievers thinks that the toy is absolutely the most amazing thing they have ever seen. You tickle him, and he goes crazy. He sits, rolls on the floor, lies on his back kicking, rolls around and rights himself to, amazingly, a standing position only to fall on the floor laughing again. At a price of around $40.00, it is an investment to be made, not only because it is probably the cutest toy I have seen in my entire 53 years of life, it's also one of the most sophisticated. And, aside from toy robots of the 1990s with wagging tail metallic dogs and highly annoying Furbies who border less on being entertaining and more on populating a child's nursery with something akin to a possessed paperweight, the T.M.X. Elmo is absolutely unequalled. Buy this one because it is prototypical, the first of its kind. He represents a whole new world of toys about to open up for a new generation. But more importantly, he passes the truest test of all for a toy collector's scrutiny… he is just an absolutely remarkable toy. So, as we wrap up our 100 years of looking at toys, I will make a few predictions as to what may be hot in the future, and what you should consider adding to any general classic toy collection. I'm not an investment counselor, and certainly some toys appreciate in value better than real estate and stocks, and others fall by the wayside for a general lack of interest. But, for what it's worth, here are the hot tips from a toy collector who has been out there in the real world of collecting for 33 years, now concluding what is his eighth book for Collector Books.

Dave's HOT TIPS for FUTURE Toy Collecting!

1. Buy popular toys of television and movie characters who have had a life span of at least 10 years. If they have survived for a decade, a generation or two later will remember them.
2. Buy unique toys which reflect transportation trends of today. Look for unusual interpretations of common toys. If you are going to purchase a model train set, purchase the one with the less common, rarer, or more limited edition engine.
3. Buy toys with boxes that are graphic and unusual, especially ones that show a design far beyond simply picturing the toy itself.
4. If you go to a toy store and see a nearly empty shelf with only one remaining diecast car or one remaining action figure, buy the single one that is left. I know that this advice sounds odd, but the popularity that made the toy scarce on the shelf now will make it even more desirable in the future because it is the popular model or version, and after all those that are consumed and played with are lost, worn out, or broken, yours will still be mint and in the box.
5. Buy toys that are the first of their kind, like the T.M.X., Tickle Me Elmo.
6. Buy new toys that represent new technology. But make sure that maintaining them (with strange types of expensive batteries or odd rechargers) won't be a problem for the long haul.

7. Limit the size and scope of your new acquisitions so that you don't eventually have to "dump" your collection onto the market at a yard sale or flea market just to make space.
8. Buy boxed toy examples of famous sports figures, political figures, or celebrities that you think will have a future, toys in the likeness of people you think will have a lasting cultural significance.
9. Never buy limited editions of any toy just because they are limited. Manufacturers aren't stupid. Editions are usually "limited" to exactly the amount of supply a manufacturer believes will sell.
10. And, most important of all… buy what you like. Chances are if you liked a new toy now as a grown up, it will appeal to another collector in yet another generation in 30 years or so. There is something universal about the classic appeal of a smartly designed, colorful, and unique toy… new or old.

T.M.X Elmo by Fisher Price, most popular toy of 2005 – 2006, $35.00 – 60.00.

T.M.X Elmo by Fisher Price, closeup of face and box with decals. $35.00 – 60.00.

Sesame Street large plastic windup car, 1990s, $25.00 – 35.00.

Ernie from Sesame Street, lever action windup car, 1990s, $25.00 – 35.00.

Big Bird from Sesame Street, fun fire truck, 1990s, $25.00 – 35.00.

Sesame Street wallet from Sesame Place Park, 1990s, $10.00 – 15.00.

Ernie from Sesame Street, plastic windup drummer, 8", 1980s, $30.00 – 45.00.

Ty Beanie Baby, dalmation, with original hang tag, $10.00 – 15.00.

Ty Beanie Baby, frog, with original hang tag, $10.00 – 15.00.

Ty Beanie Baby "Peace," with hang tang, $25.00 – 40.00.

Ty Beanie Baby, "Erin," with original hang tag, $50.00 – 75.00.

Ty Beanie Baby, "Maple," with original hang tag, $35.00 – 50.00.

Ty Beanie Baby, "Britannia," with original hang tag, $50.00 – 75.00.

Ty Beanie Baby, "Diana," with original hang tag, $55.00 – 90.00.

Puffalumps, two versions of rabbit, by Fisher Price, pair, no box, $25.00 – 40.00.

Puffalumps rabbit by Fisher Price, in original box, 1980s, $40.00 – 65.00.

Puffalumps rabbits holding eggs, by Fisher Price, pair, no box, $25.00 – 40.00.

My Little Pony, purple, 1990s, $12.00 – 20.00.

My Little Pony pink haired figure, 1990s, $12.00 – 20.00.

My Little Pony, pink, 1990s, $12.00 – 20.00.

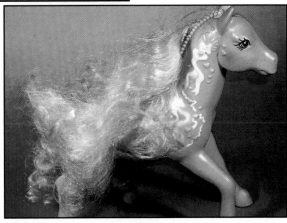

Fraggle Rock child's meal toys, Premium Toys, pair, 1980s, $20.00 – 30.00.

Fraggle Rock child's meal toy, Premium Toys, 1980s, $10.00 – 15.00.

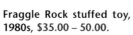

Fraggle Rock stuffed toy, 1980s, $35.00 – 50.00.

Snoopy Aviva diecast metal toy biplane,
in original box, $40.00 – 65.00.

Snoopy Aviva diecast metal toy car, in original box,
$35.00 – 60.00.

Snoopy small plush toy,
recent, $12.00 – 18.00.

Snoopy plastic push
puppet, $15.00 – 30.00.

Mickey and Minnie small plush figures, recent, pair, $20.00 – 35.00.

Mickey and Minnie Mouse plastic windup, by Schilling, recent, $20.00 – 25.00.

Minnie Mouse as the Easter bunny, plush toy, recent, $15.00 – 25.00.

Mickey Mouse riding Pluto windup, by Schilling, recent, $20.00 – 30.00.

Walt Disney's Classic Collection, set of three Pinocchio figures, $300.00 – 500.00.

An American Tail mouse, plastic, 4", $10.00 – 15.00.

Disney's Dinosaur, recent, from WDW, $10.00 – 15.00.

Disney's Snow White Dwarfs Coal Mine Train set, three cars,
$30.00 – 40.00.

Disney's *Lion King* figures, recent, $8.00 – 12.00 each.

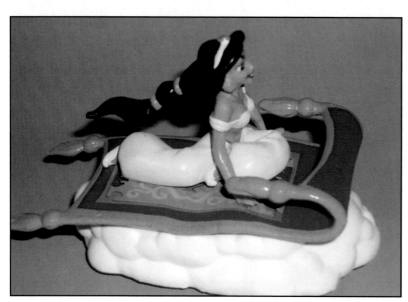

Jasmine on carpet windup
toy, 1990s, $10.00 – 15.00.

Disney's *Aladdin* toys and figures, $8.00 – 12.00 each.

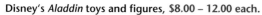

Disney's *Aladdin* toys, $20.00 – 35.00 doll; $5.00 – 10.00 each figure.

Disney's *Aladdin* and Jasmine action figures, 1990s, $15.00 – 25.00 pair.

Peter Pan and Captain Hook snow globe, recent, $20.00 – 35.00.

Troll, vinyl doll with original clothes, 1990s, $10.00 – 20.00.

Figment from Epcot, PVC figure, 1990s, $10.00 – 15.00.

Alf, from popular television show, 4", PVC, 1980s, $8.00 – 12.00.

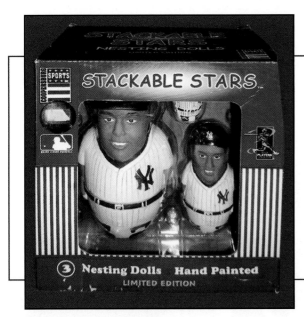

Stackable Stars Derek Jeter, Yankees dolls in box, $15.00 – 25.00.

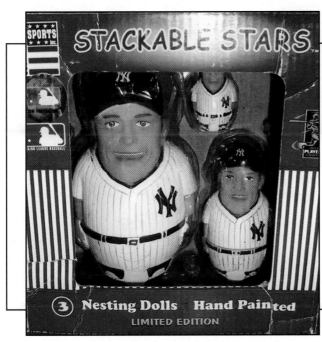

Stackable Stars Jason Giambi, Yankees dolls in box, $15.00 – 25.00.

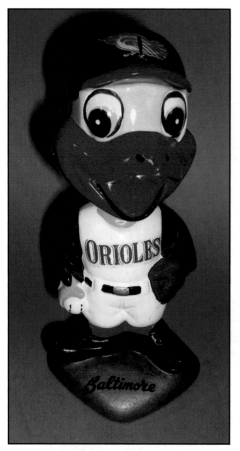

Baltimore Orioles bobble head, souvenir
figure, $45.00 – 65.00.

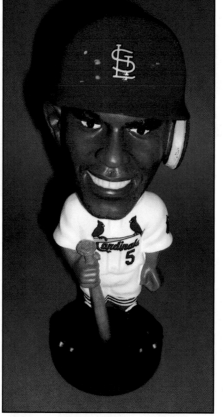

St. Louis Cardinals bobble head, Pujols
figure, $45.00 – 65.00.

St. Louis Cardinals bobble head, Edmonds
figure, $45.00 – 65.00.

Teddy bear with little dog, recent reproduction, by Midwest, $25.00 – 35.00.

Bugs Bunny with Elmer Fudd radio, plastic, $40.00 – 65.00.

Smokey Bear pail/ashtray, $15.00 – 25.00.

Rainforest Café child's vinyl toys, recent, $3.00. – 4.00 each.

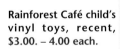

Rainforest Café child's vinyl toys, recent, $3.00. – 4.00 each.

Fisher Price See 'N Say, in original box, recent, $7.00 – 15.00.

Lost in Space robot, windup, 1990s, recent reproduction, 4", $15.00 – 30.00.

Lost in Space robot, built up model, recent reproduction, $35.00 – 50.00.

Ford Mustang diecast car, 8", metal and plastic, recent, $25.00 – 35.00.

Small Ford Mustang diecast car, 4" long, very detailed, $15.00 – 20.00.

Ford Mustang diecast car, in original box, by MIRA, recent, $30.00 – 40.00.

Standard sedan convertible, in original box, $125.00 – 165.00.

Matchbox Models of Yesteryear Horsham steam engine, $55.00 – 95.00.

Matchbox fire pumper with hoses, recent, $45.00 – 65.00.

Matchbox Models of Yesteryear Garden City fire truck, $45.00 – 65.00.

Matchbox Clayton Fire Brigade with Santa and Mrs. Claus, $50.00 – 75.00.

Matchbox Springfield Fire Brigade support vehicle, $45.00 – 65.00.

Matchbox White Mountain National Forest diecast truck, $45.00 – 75.00.

Christie pumper truck, model of 1900s, by Johnny Lightning, $35.00 – 55.00.

Matchbox 1900s pumper, scale model, rare, $100.00 – 150.00.

Matchbox pumper truck, horseless antique pumper, $85.00 – 125.00.

Matchbox Models of Yesteryear horsedrawn pumper, $100.00 – 160.00.

Matchbox diecast and detailed horse drawn brigade with riders, $125.00 – 175.00.

Matchbox Models of Yesteryear antique fire truck, highly detailed, $65.00 – 95.00.

Matchbox Models of Yesteryear pumper truck, 4" long, $75.00 – 100.00.

Matchbox Models of Yesteryear antique white fire truck, $75.00 – 100.00.

Matchbox Models of Yesteryear ladder and hose truck, $65.00 – 85.00.

Collector's Guide

(Note: An abbreviated version of this chapter also appears in David Longest's *Collecting Dsneyana* also published in the fall of 2007. The full chapter appears here in its absolute entirety because of its importance to toy collection acquisition, maintenance, and guidance.)

This chapter is intended to be an aid for toy collectors of all ages and levels who might need a little additional information in regard to maintaining a toy collection and expanding it. There are really two parts to this chapter. Part one deals with toy maintenance and preservation and part two deals with expanding your collection. Even though I have been a writer for many toy publications over the past 30 years, I am first and foremost a collector. The writing is a part time profession and a hobby. The collecting of old toys is a passion. Like my three golden retrievers who constantly roam about the house with "things" in their mouths and who continually bring things to me when they don't even know why they do it, I collect things. I am not even sure why. And the things I collect are old toys.

One of the first considerations of any collector, advanced or novice, is "Where am I going to put all these toys!?" That's an interesting question which poses all kinds of pitfalls and possibilities. Most collectors don't purchase antique toy treasures just to hide them away; they usually purchase toys to display them. Collecting may bring the collector great adventure in the field, but ultimately it's the visual aspect of acquiring old toys that is so satisfying. We like to look at them. Museum curators learned long, long ago that heavy glass is a friend of the historian. Glass keeps danger from people, insects, dust, and even light out, and it keeps the items behind it safe and sound. Invest in glass. Buy cases with glass fronts that have solid closures. Buy all the glass front shelves and storage cases you can afford, even if it means sacrificing some toy purchases from time to time. Your collection will be the better for it. Glass is the toy collector's greatest friend. So is proper lighting. Lighting for collectibles is wonderful when it is built into fine display cabinets, but watch the temperature. Today's halogen lights burn very warm, and I have seen well meaning collectors put highly prized and valuable dolls on the top shelf of a halogen lit cabinet only to return and find cracked and damaged composition dolls that were literally baked in the hot oven of the display case. If a toy has even the remotest possibility of being damaged by heat, don't put it near the internal or recessed lighting of a display cabinet.

In addition to lighting concerns regarding cabinetry for display, collectors should also consider access. Some showcases are built for easy access with magnetic catches on the front that just require a single push and a full door panel swings open. Other clever configurations of display cabinetry have rear access available so that front glass panels are not marred by hinges or latches. Rear access is fine for display cabinets as long as you have access to the rear. A rear access door for toy shelving is useless if a collector has to pull the entire display case out from the wall to access the rear entry doors. Most collectors prefer direct front hinged doors, or those with "invisible" side hinging glass doors. Both allow for easy access for cleaning, show and tell, and maintenance access for your antique toys.

Directional light from above and just slightly in front of a showcase is a wonderful way to light old toys. Collectors who know me well know that I am a theatre teacher and director by profession, and believe me, I know lighting. The old textbook adage of "Forty five degrees up and out" has always worked well in the theatre, meaning the 45 degree front lighting angle is perfect for illumination of actors upon a stage (or toys inside a showcase). That 45 degree angle allows for full illumination from the front and above, but it's just the right angle to eliminate glare from the glass in front. It's a perfect geometric balance of light and design. Try it. Install some strip lighting out and in front of your best showcases. You will be amazed at the results. A collection of antique toys can literally come to life when lit properly.

In just the same way that light can be a collector's friend, it can also be an enemy. I have learned this lesson the hard way. Over the years, I have kept many of my best antique toy lithographed games and books on display on open shelves high on the walls. None of these are in direct line of light from the sun as a full length front porch shades our entire house and all the front exposure windows. Just the same, plenty of ultra violet light filters into our house indirectly, and over a 10 to 15 year period, some of my finest antique toy games and lithographed books have slowly faded to less than attractive colors. One particularly horrifying lesson I learned concerned a rare Mickey Mouse Pop Gun Set that I purchased some 25 years ago and paid a dear price for. I purchased it for around $450.00 in the early 1980s and proudly displayed this impressive piece high on a shelf (not behind glass) just around the corner from an indirectly sunlit window. I repeat, it was indirect sunlight. The game never (even in the summer) was exposed to direct sunlight, just bright indirect sun an hour or two a day. A couple of years ago, I took the game down to dust it, and over a decade and a half, the deep green background of this beautiful game manufactured by Marks Brothers of Boston, Massachusetts, in the 1930s had gradually faded to an ugly light pea green right before my eyes. And the damage was so steady and so gradual, I had not even noticed it. I sold the game to a buyer who was aware of the damage for around $300.00, but the target set would have been worth around $1,000.00 today. Aside from being an important $700.00 lesson, it was a real tragedy for the toy. And it was my own fault.

Sunlight is the greatest enemy of toys. I repeat and will capitalize it, SUNLIGHT IS THE GREATEST ENEMY OF TOYS! It is far more damaging than rust, because ultraviolet light damage creeps up on the toy and can never be reversed. Rust can be stopped, halted. There is no cure for ultraviolet light damage and its ugly fading effects upon old lithography of both tin and paper toys is relentless. Keep your toys behind glass which helps reflect away ultraviolet light and keep them away from even indirectly sunlit windows. May my $700.00 mistake save your own collection's value.

Now, back to the glass. Make sure showcases have a tight seal, and if insects like dust mites or moths are a problem in your particular climate, make sure you keep them away from your toys. Moths don't just like wool, they love old glue present in composition toys and paper lithographed books and boxes. They suck up glue soaked pulp like it was turkey and gravy on Thanksgiving. After a lengthy summer vacation one year, I returned in horror to find that one single moth had devoured the complete soles of the felt shoes of a Doc the Dwarf (from Disney's Snow White) doll that I owned, had eaten up his wool beard until all that was left was a wool stubble and then for dessert had crunched away on the glue soaked composition nose of the doll. Thankfully, the moth had expired from over eating and was dead at the dwarf's feet. He didn't damage any of the other dolls in the case. But if he hadn't died, he would have. They are stinky and unpleasant, but a single moth ball in the back of that showcase will prevent such dreaded moments. Be on guard.

Regarding storage of paper items, make sure you use archival worthy products. Acid-free papers and inert plastics that won't melt or interact with antique inks and paper pulps are available at fine scrapbooking and stationary stores. Even comic book dealers know the merits of proper paper storage so seek these dealers out if there is one in your area. Anyone who knows about paper preservation can be helpful, and unless you are a museum curator or an archeologist, you need help. Make sure books are sealed off from insects, humidity, and extreme heat. Remember that such toy materials as rubber, paper, wool, and wood are all organic, and nothing organic lasts forever. It's a scientific fact. But proper preservation methods now can extend the life of antique toys when they are given care.

A key word to mention here is preservation, not restoration. Restoration is needed when a toy is purchased that needs serious repair, and preservation is the management technique administered so that eventual restoration is never needed. So remember: Preservation, not restoration. Keep those words in mind and your collection will have a long life.

So, why not restoration? Aren't restored toys nicer to look at and more stable in the long haul once they are brought back up to speed? Yes, they are. But once restored, always restored. Watch any episode of the popular PBS series *Antiques Roadshow* and you will quickly learn what restoration does to the value of any antique. Toys are certainly no exception. Yes, restoration makes badly damaged toys nicer to look at, and yes, restoration will help preserve them. But it is a fact of life in the collecting world that collectors prefer not to purchase restorations. The problem is, it is often difficult to discern where restoration begins and ends. Is a toy a total repaint example, or just partial repaint? Does it have all new replacement parts or just a few? A toy that needs no conditional apologies is a toy that rests cleaner on the conscience of its owner. Buy a toy that is in 100% original excellent condition, and that's a toy you will never have to buy again. Buy mint condition when you can afford it, and you never have to buy again. If a toy goes into your collection as mint, it is impossible to need an upgrade. You have saved yourself big dollars in the long run since you don't have to load and unload toy examples by trading and upgrading and re-trading only to find yet a better example later. Buy mint and you buy once. So, avoid restorations, and buy mint toys whenever you can possibly afford them. Your collection (and your sanity) will be all the better for it!

Another commonly overlooked aspect of maintaining a successful collection throughout many decades is insurance. Nearly every collector in America lives within an area of some major disaster threat, be it hurricanes, earthquakes, fire, flood, or even tornadoes. Toy collections don't last under any of these circumstances, and theft is an even greater threat. Make sure your insurance riders on your home owner's policies are up to date to keep pace with the growth of your collecting habits. Most standard home owner's policies offer little or no replacement values for collectibles… those have to be protected and provided for with additional insurance riders and loads of documentation, but in the long run it is worth it. If you are willing to sink thousands of dollars annually into collecting antique toys, then surely it is worth several hundred dollars a year to protect yourself from significant financial loss should the unthinkable happen. And keep good records. Video record your entire collection, case by case and wall to wall. It may seem ridiculous as you are doing it, but realize that in the event of a natural disaster or a major theft, it will be important to be able to reconstruct what your collection looked like once upon a time. If you won't do it for yourself, do it for me. As an author who benefited from your purchase of this book, let me repay you by telling you to insure your collection today. There is no rational excuse for any other course of action. You must protect the investment you have made in your toys. Do it now! No excuses.

So, the checklist includes insure, display behind glass, avoid ultraviolet light, preserve but don't restore, light properly and safely, and one more thing — control moisture. One of the worst places to keep a collection is in a lower level room or basement that is subject to moisture. If you must keep the toys down there, control the humidity with continuous use of dehumidifiers. If you can't control the moisture problems in a basement or lower level, then move the toys. Rust works more quickly than ultraviolet light and its devastating effects upon tin lithographed toys is unavoidable. Even waxing tin toys won't help them if they are continually subject to humid air. Keep your books and your toys as dry as you possibly can. They will last longer, and so will your investment (and your sanity).

So, now that we have covered how to maintain your collection, let's discuss how to expand it. First and foremost, know your economics. If buying antique toys is putting your family seriously in debt, your collection won't last. Eventually you will find yourself "dumping" your collection into the marketplace to pay off debts and that's a quick way to lose what you have worked so hard to find. Slow and steady are the key words here. Buy mint condition toys when you can afford them, and if you can't buy mint, don't buy at all. Save for the next opportunity when you can buy mint. It takes will power and discipline to come home empty handed from an antique toy show or auction, but if it means not putting yourself in the precarious situation of buying old toys you didn't have the money for in the first place, then the pain of walking away is misery justified for a lesson well learned. Buy mint when you can afford it, and don't buy anything else when you can't afford mint.

A small, pristine mint collection of old toys is worth far more than a whole house filled with worn out, damaged junk. The internet has opened up incredible possibilities for today's toy collector. Nearly everybody knows how to shop and sell on eBay now, but five years ago this was the exception and not the rule. Buying habits are volatile now, and as eBay's slogan continually reinforces, you can find it whenever you want it or need it, whatever it is. In the world of toy collecting, it is the next toy you just have to have for your collection. Learn the ins and outs of internet buying and make sure you have a recourse for a fouled-up purchase. It's buyer beware with most internet purchases, but eBay's user feedback system allows for a spirit of honesty and cooperation to exist between buyer and seller on good days. But be forewarned: It can be very difficult to take action against a deal that has gone sour. If you live in New York City and your seller is in San Francisco, it's going to be tough to actually litigate if a real problem exists. Normally, bidders and buyers and sellers work through problems in a virtual spirit of cooperation trying to resolve problems for the common good. At least, that's the way eBay and everyone else hopes it will work.

Be patient as you bid, learn to use bidding strategies that are open and honest, not cut-throat. "Snipers" often lie in wait out there in cyberland just waiting to outbid you in the last seconds, so understand the eBay and other internet site rules of the game, and then learn to play the game successfully. In the past eight years, a substantial portion of my own collecting has been through eBay and internet purchases, and less has been from attending antique toy shows… and I miss that. Regardless of how much you love your computer, it will never replace the human link and satisfaction of building trust with live dealers at real antique shows. Nothing will ever replace that. So don't overlook the people out there who can put you in touch with great toys. They still exist. How do you find them? Read on.

The most commonly overlooked successful means of finding great antique toys is word of mouth. It seems so simple it looks ridiculous on the surface, but it works. Talk about what you collect to everyone you meet. You never know what people have hiding in their closets… really. Just last month, I was bemoaning the fact that there was one toy that had eluded me all these years, a Beany character doll made by Mattel in the early 1960s and a toy I wanted badly on Christmas morning in 1960. Usually Santa brought everything I wanted, I was a particularly young lad and I communicated to Santa my wishes, down to even crayons and batteries when I needed them. But somehow in 1960, either I or Santa, or both of us slipped up. There was no Beany. (In later years, I came to believe that my Dad may have seen Beany as a doll, and he didn't want me to have a doll. But I will never know for sure.) Anyway, I was whining to an antique dealer friend that I am now 53, have just recovered from quintuple heart by-pass surgery nine months ago, and I "Still don't have my Beany." Now this sounds ridiculous (and is!) except for the fact that I was being honest and had always avoided buying one because those darn little dolls are always missing their cute propellers on top. I told my good friend my woes, and three days later, she found one at a half-off post holiday sale in absolute mint condition at the local D.A.V. thrift store. I mean, the little guy is just-off-the-store-shelf-like-in-1960 mint! She bought him so "right" that she just gave him to me! (Probably to end my whining!)

So, as I sit here in my study typing away on my Dell, Beany is now smiling his quirky grin and staring at me. But, I've got him. And for some really odd reason, I feel better because he is here. Maybe it's my mortality that I'm facing because of the heart surgery, or maybe it's my blood pressure medicine kicking in, but I would swear that both he knows and I know we were eventually supposed to end up together. But I had to wait nearly 47 years! I use this illustration to drive home the point that you need to talk to everyone whom you meet (and trust) that toy collecting is an important part of your life. As you share, and they share, you will be amazed at what unusual antique toys might just "emerge" from the shadows of old basements, attics, garages, and closets. Somebody you know may have just what you are looking for. Don't be shy. Talk about your toys.

How else can you expand your toy horizons? Don't overlook the power of the country auction on a bad weather day. If the crowd is down, so may be the prices. Elmer and Viola Reynolds of Indiana who contributed many toys from their wonderful collections to this book once headed to a remote country auction on a snowy day and left a bid on the Mickey Mouse Marks Brothers Piano mint in a mint box. I believe their left bid was around $200.00, and it won the toy. Even on a bad day, the piano should have brought $1,000.00 two decades ago. Now it is worth thousands. And they have it all because they went to that auction when the weather was lousy.

Yard sales produce wonderful toys, too, if (and that's a big if) you are lucky enough to be the first guy there. It's worth a shot, but it's a long shot. And yard sale scouring eats up tanks of gas with very few treasures ever

found. Certainly huge outdoor antique extravaganzas like the annual ones held in Springfield, Ohio, each year still draw thousands of dealers and tens of thousands of buyers. Brimfield Summer Shows in Brimfield, Massachusetts, are still a happy hunting ground for wonderful antique toys, but under priced bargains are getting harder and harder to find there. There's just so much competition now. The year round St. Charles Toy Shows billed as the Antique Toy and Doll World Shows are still worth a weekend in northern Illinois, but the rare stuff seems to have already been discovered decades ago. The internet seems to have changed everything… or has it?

What may have really changed is what we are looking for. When I was in my twenties, I looked for that toy that I thought was under priced and rare. In my thirties, I looked for that which was just rare. In my forties, I looked for whatever I thought would be a toy I might not ever see again, and now that I am in my fifties, I am always looking to find… my shoes. It is all a matter of timing and perspectives.

As older advanced collectors maintain their collections for decades, all the while wondering what will become of their toys when they are gone, they start to drift philosophical. They can either make preparations for their own families to inherit boxes and cases of playthings, or make provisions for a museum to be the future beneficiary. Whatever the choice, families need to be kept informed as to both the value of the toys in a collection, and the individual provenance of the toys as each is acquired. Every toy has a history, and unless the wise collector gathers that personal history as an antique toy is purchased, it will most likely be lost forever.

Consider the case of Francis West. She was a child in the early 1930s and born in the late 1920s. I knew nothing of her, until my own toy collecting fate entertwined with her own story. (A favorite toy of her childhood was a small Mickey Mouse tin pail by Ohio Art — it's pictured on page 89.) By the time I got to know who Francis was, she had already passed away. On a given Saturday morning some 12 years ago, the estate sale of Francis West was held in the East Highlands of Louisville, Kentucky. I missed the sale, or more particularly, missed hearing about it. The sale took place around Labor Day, and I heard about the Francis West sale about one week after the fact. There was talk at the Louisville Stewart's Labor Day Holiday Flea Market regarding a great sale with great toys, and in particular, a rare Mickey Mouse Disney pail by Ohio Art. The pail was purchased at the sale by a casual collector friend, and it was a particular small variety of an Ohio Art pail I had never heard of: 3" tall Mickey on the boat dock with Pluto and Minnie in a canoe. I have still never seen this pail pictured in anyone's book (until now) and it is the belief among advanced collectors and Ohio Art fanatics that this pail may have been produced only one year and included only with the rare Mickey Mouse fishing set. Anyway, one week later, my detective work began. I approached my friend Mike and offered to trade him for the pail. At the time, I owned a rare Mickey Mouse Nifty Mechanical Drummer that I had purchased for several hundred dollars years before, and I eventually traded Mike for that rare pail, plus he added some cash back into the deal since the Mickey drummer was worth about $3,000.00 at the time. Flash back in time to the Stewart's Labor Day show when I was just hearing about the pail. As I walked through several different toy dealer's booths, the talk was still of the Francis West sale. There were dolls, pristine doll furniture, books, games… you name it! And all this "new" old merchandise had been purchased at the West auction. As I scanned one dealer's shelves, I struck gold. Upon a shelf were photographs, large black and white photographs, of little girls standing under Christmas trees. I asked the dealer where the pictures of the little girls came from and she answered, to no surprise "the Francis West auction." Then it struck me. I laid out the five pictures side by side and realized that the large black and white photos weren't of five different little girls at Christmas, they were five consecutive Christmas morning photos of a cute little girl, growing year by year. What I had in front of me was a visual record of the Christmas mornings from the childhood of Francis West! And in each photograph was a wealth of toys. I bought every picture in the stack, knowing that this was an incredible record of 1930s toy history, not to mention a perfect history of the childhood of Francis West. Then another thought struck me — as I scanned the dealer's

shelves, I saw a doll vanity in the photograph before me, and there was the exact same vanity on the shelf. In the photograph was a Bakelite and celluloid child's brush, comb, and miniature doll grooming set, on the dealer's shelf was the exact same set! Okay, I had to take a deep breath. For a collector, it just doesn't get any better than this. I was able to purchase toys from the auction of Miss West (she was an only child and never married and was originally from Cincinnati, Ohio) along with the original photographs of those toys when they were brand new under the Christmas tree. This has been a long story, but it is a prime example of collecting the provenance (the written or oral history of a toy) at the time of purchase. Whenever you can collect the story of the toy when you acquire it, you not only add significantly to its value, you add remarkably to its history. Don't ever forget to ask about the family history of a toy when you first purchase it. This toy collecting hobby can be exhausting, tiring, sometimes fruitless, and even frustrating.

But, we stay on the hunt for those great old toys, don't we? Why? Maybe it is genetic. Some switch in our brain has clicked on and we don't know how to switch it off. Like my golden retrievers, we run after our toys because we find joy in just bringing them back, for no apparent reason. And tomorrow, we will do the same all over again…. just because it is fun, and feels good.

You can learn a lot from watching your dogs. Beany-is still smiling at me, and my goldens are each chomping on a squishy toy… all three of them. We are all four of us true collectors, and we still don't know why. But it's still fun. Life is good.

Enjoy your days of collecting in the time you have left!

— David Longest, December 2007

About the Author

David Longest is the author of six previous books on collecting antique toys published by Collector Books: *Character Toys and Collectibles* (1984), *Character Toys and Collectibles, Series Two* (1986), *Toys — Antique and Collectible* (1988), *The Collector's Encyclopedia of Disneyana* (with Michael Stern, 1991), *Antique Toys — 1870 to 1960* (1993), and *Cartoon Toys and Collectibles* (1997). For 2007, two new books by Longest will be released: *Collecting Disneyana* (2007) and *The Toy Yearbook* (2007). David is proud to have been a Collector Books author for over a quarter of a century!

Longest has written nationally for *Collector's Showcase Magazine*, *Antique Trader Magazine*, the *Tri-State Trader*, *Antique Toy World Magazine*, and he served as a monthly feature writer and contributing editor for *Toy Shop Magazine* in the 1990s.

David's full time job is serving as a teacher and director of theatre at New Albany High School in Indiana where he is an award winning teacher with an award winning theatre program. His program was awarded the National Outstanding High School Theatre Award by the Educational Theatre Association in 2004 and Longest was selected as the New Albany Floyd County Teacher of the Year and an Indiana Teacher of the Year Semi-Finalist also in 2004. David is additionally the recipient of two Lilly Endowment Teacher Creativity Awards and the WHAS-TV Excel Award for Outstanding Teaching. Longest is also one of the only high school teachers in the nation to ever win the prestigious National American History Medal awarded by the D.A.R. in Washington, D.C. which he won for co-authoring an original musical on Lewis and Clark and his adaptation of *Little Women* which was published by Dramatic Publishing of Chicago, Illinois. Longest has been a guest lecturer on Broadway in New York for Broadway Classroom, and he and his students were featured in three full pages of *The New York Times* in May of 2005. Additionally, David Longest and his students are soon to be featured in a 2008 motion picture documentary release by Lions Gate Pictures of Hollywood directed by film director Barry Blaustein devoted to exemplary high school musical theatre programs. Most recently, Longest was selected by Music Theatre International and Walt Disney Theatricals to be one of very few pilot premiere directors in the nation to produce an early production of Disney's *High School Musical* which will be featured at the International Thespian Festival this year in Lincoln, Nebraska. David's former students have appeared in nearly two dozen Broadway, London West End, and American national theatre tours. David has been a teacher for 30 years.

Longing for more information on toys... check out this newest book from David Longest!

Collecting Disneyana is exactly the book its title suggests — a book all about the fun of collecting objects related to Walt Disney characters and movies. The book presents extensive examples of very early Disneyana in a chapter titled The Golden Years, specializing in Disney's "fab five": early Mickey Mouse, Minnie Mouse, Donald Duck, Goofy, and Pluto. Later chapters include The Feature Films, highlighting collectibles from *Bambi, Pinocchio, Snow White and the Seven Dwarfs, Dumbo,* and a host of other Disney films; and The Television Years highlights collectibles from the 1950s and 1960s including The Mickey Mouse Club and Disney's Wonderful World of Color. Finally, the book brings collectors right up to date with an informative chapter on Recent and Future Collectibles which showcases collectibles from Winnie the Pooh to Beauty and the Beast and also highlights the current Disneyana craze of pin collecting. Advanced collectors of Disneyana will appreciate some never before published photos of extremely rare Disneyana, and newer collectors will be excited about the substantial collecting tips offered. This impressive volume contains over 950 photos with reliable values and is an absolute must for any fan of Disney memorabilia!

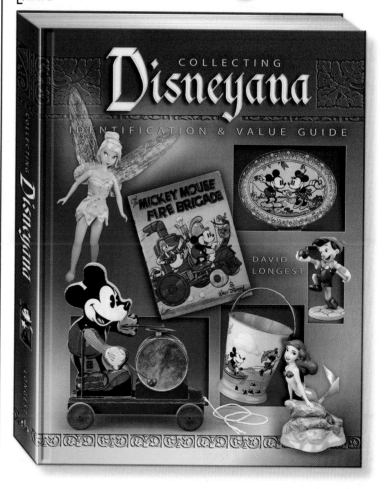

more great TITLES from collector books

DOLLS

6315	American Character Dolls, Izen	$24.95
7346	Barbie Doll Around the World, 1964 – 2007, Augustyniak	$29.95
2079	Barbie Doll Fashion, Volume I, Eames	$24.95
4846	Barbie Doll Fashion, Volume II, Eames	$24.95
6319	Barbie Doll Fashion, Volume III, Eames	$29.95
6546	Collector's Ency. of Barbie Doll Exclusives & More, 3rd Ed., Augustyniak	$29.95
6920	Collector's Encyclopedia of American Composition Dolls, Volume I, Mertz	$29.95
6451	Collector's Encyclopedia of American Composition Dolls, Volume II, Mertz	$29.95
6636	Collector's Encyclopedia of Madame Alexander Dolls, Crowsey	$24.95
6456	Collector's Guide to Dolls of the 1960s and 1970s, Volume II, Sabulis	$24.95
6944	The Complete Guide to Shirley Temple Dolls and Collectibles, Bervaldi-Camaratta	$29.95
7028	Doll Values, Antique to Modern, 9th Edition, Edward	$14.95
6467	Paper Dolls of the 1960s, 1970s, and 1980s, Nichols	$24.95
6642	20th Century Paper Dolls, Young	$19.95

TOYS & MARBLES

2333	Antique & Collectible Marbles, 3rd Edition, Grist	$9.95
6649	Big Book of Toy Airplanes, Miller	$24.95
6938	Everett Grist's Big Book of Marbles, 3rd Edition	$24.95
7523	Breyer Animal Collector's Gde., 5th Ed., Browell/Korber-Weimer/Kesicki	$24.95
7356	Collector's Guide to Housekeeping Toys, Wright	$16.95
7355	Hot Wheels, The Ultimate Redline Guide Companion, Clark/Wicker	$29.95
6466	Matchbox Toys, 1947 to 2003, 4th Edition, Johnson	$24.95
7539	Schroeder's Collectible Toys, Antique to Modern Price Guide, 11th Ed.	$19.95
6638	The Other Matchbox Toys, 1947 to 2004, Johnson	$19.95
6650	Toy Car Collector's Guide, 2nd Edition, Johnson	$24.95

JEWELRY, WATCHES & PURSES

4704	Antique & Collectible Buttons, Wisniewski	$19.95
4850	Collectible Costume Jewelry, Simonds	$24.95
5675	Collectible Silver Jewelry, Rezazadeh	$24.95
6468	Collector's Ency. of Pocket & Pendant Watches, 1500 – 1950, Bell	$24.95
6554	Coro Jewelry, Brown	$29.95
7529	Costume Jewelry 101, 2nd Edition, Carroll	$24.95
7025	Costume Jewelry 202, Carroll	$24.95
4940	Costume Jewelry, A Practical Handbook & Value Guide, Rezazadeh	$24.95
5812	Fifty Years of Collectible Fashion Jewelry, 1925 – 1975, Baker	$24.95
6330	Handkerchiefs: A Collector's Guide, Guarnaccia/Guggenheim	$24.95
6833	Handkerchiefs: A Collector's Guide, Volume II, Guarnaccia/Guggenheim	$24.95
6464	Inside the Jewelry Box, Pitman	$24.95
7358	Inside the Jewelry Box, Volume 2, Pitman	$24.95
5695	Ladies' Vintage Accessories, Johnson	$24.95
1181	100 Years of Collectible Jewelry, 1850 – 1950, Baker	$9.95
6645	100 Years of Purses, 1880s to 1980s, Aikins	$24.95
6942	Rhinestone Jewelry: Figurals, Animals, and Whimsicals, Brown	$24.95

6039	Signed Beauties of Costume Jewelry, Brown	$24.95
6341	Signed Beauties of Costume Jewelry, Volume II, Brown	$24.95
6555	20th Century Costume Jewelry, Aikins	$24.95
5620	Unsigned Beauties of Costume Jewelry, Brown	$24.95

ARTIFACTS, GUNS, KNIVES, & TOOLS

1868	Antique Tools, Our American Heritage, McNerney	$9.95
6822	Antler, Bone & Shell Artifacts, Hothem	$24.95
1426	Arrowheads & Projectile Points, Hothem	$7.95
5355	Cattaraugus Cutlery Co., Stewart/Ritchie	$19.95
6231	Indian Artifacts of the Midwest, Book V, Hothem	$24.95
7037	Modern Guns, Identification & Values, 16th Ed., Quertermous	$16.95
7034	Ornamental Indian Artifacts, Hothem	$34.95
6567	Paleo-Indian Artifacts, Hothem	$29.95
6569	Remington Knives, Past & Present, Stewart/Ritchie	$16.95
7366	Standard Guide to Razors, 3rd Edition, Stewart/Ritchie	$12.95
7035	Standard Knife Collector's Guide, 5th Edition, Ritchie/Stewart	$16.95

PAPER COLLECTIBLES & BOOKS

6623	Collecting American Paintings, James	$29.95
7039	Collecting Playing Cards, Pickvet	$24.95
6826	Collecting Vintage Children's Greeting Cards, McPherson	$24.95
6553	Collector's Guide to Cookbooks, Daniels	$24.95
1441	Collector's Guide to Post Cards, Wood	$9.95
6627	Early 20th Century Hand-Painted Photography, Ivankovich	$24.95
6936	Leather Bound Books, Boutiette	$24.95
7036	Old Magazine Advertisements, 1890 – 1950, Clear	$24.95
6940	Old Magazines, 2nd Edition, Clear	$19.95
3973	Sheet Music Reference & Price Guide, 2nd Ed., Pafik/Guiheen	$19.95
6837	Vintage Postcards for the Holidays, 2nd Edition, Reed	$24.95

GLASSWARE

7362	American Pattern Glass Table Sets, Florence/Cornelius/Jones	$24.95
6930	Anchor Hocking's Fire-King & More, 3rd Ed., Florence	$24.95
7524	Coll. Glassware from the 40s, 50s & 60s, 9th Edition, Florence	$19.95
6921	Collector's Encyclopedia of American Art Glass, 2nd Edition, Shuman	$29.95
7526	Collector's Encyclopedia of Depression Glass, 18th Ed., Florence	$19.95
3905	Collector's Encyclopedia of Milk Glass, Newbound	$24.95
7026	Colors in Cambridge Glass II, Natl. Cambridge Collectors, Inc.	$29.95
7029	Elegant Glassware of the Depression Era, 12th Edition, Florence	$24.95
6334	Encyclopedia of Paden City Glass, Domitz	$29.95
3981	Evers' Standard Cut Glass Value Guide	$12.95
6126	Fenton Art Glass, 1907 – 1939, 2nd Ed., Whitmyer	$29.95
6628	Fenton Glass Made for Other Companies, Domitz	$29.95
7030	Fenton Glass Made for Other Companies, Volume II, Domitz	$29.95
6462	Florences' Glass Kitchen Shakers, 1930 – 1950s	$19.95

1.800.626.5420 Mon. – Fri. 7 am – 5 pm CT   Fax: **1.270.898.8890**

5042 Florences' Glassware Pattern Identification Guide, Vol. I $18.95
5615 Florences' Glassware Pattern Identification Guide, Vol. II $19.95
6643 Florences' Glassware Pattern Identification Guide, Vol. IV $19.95
6641 Florences' Ovenware from the 1920s to the Present $24.95
6226 Fostoria Value Guide, Long/Seate $19.95
6127 The Glass Candlestick Book, Volume 1, Akro Agate to Fenton, Felt/Stoer $24.95
6228 The Glass Candlestick Book, Volume 2, Fostoria to Jefferson, Felt/Stoer $24.95
6461 The Glass Candlestick Book, Volume 3, Kanawha to Wright, Felt/Stoer $29.95
6648 Glass Toothpick Holders, 2nd Edition, Bredehoft/Sanford..............$29.95
5827 Kitchen Glassware of the Depression Years, 6th Edition, Florence $24.95
7534 Lancaster Glass Company, 1908 –1937, Zastowney $29.95
7359 L.E. Smith Glass Company, Felt $29.95
6133 Mt. Washington Art Glass, Sisk $49.95
7027 Pocket Guide to Depression Glass & More, 15th Edition, Florence $12.95
6925 Standard Encyclopedia of Carnival Glass, 10th Ed., Edwards/Carwile $29.95
6926 Standard Carnival Glass Price Guide, 15th Ed., Edwards/Carwile $9.95
6566 Standard Encyclopedia of Opalescent Glass, 5th Ed., Edwards/Carwile $29.95
7364 Standard Encyclopedia of Pressed Glass, 5th Ed., Edwards/Carwile $29.95
6476 Westmoreland Glass, The Popular Years, 1940 – 1985, Kovar $29.95

POTTERY

6922 American Art Pottery, 2nd Edition, Sigafoose $24.95
5529 Collectible Cups & Saucers, Book II, Harran $19.95
6326 Collectible Cups & Saucers, Book III, Harran $24.95
6331 Collecting Head Vases, Barron $24.95
6943 Collecting Royal Copley, Devine................................$19.95
6621 Collector's Encyclopedia of American Dinnerware, 2nd Ed., Cunningham ...$29.95
5034 Collector's Encyclopedia of California Pottery, 2nd Ed., Chipman $24.95
6629 Collector's Encyclopedia of Fiesta, 10th Ed., Huxford $24.95
3431 Collector's Encyclopedia of Homer Laughlin China, Jasper $24.95
1276 Collector's Encyclopedia of Hull Pottery, Roberts $19.95
5609 Collector's Encyclopedia of Limoges Porcelain, 3rd Ed., Gaston $29.95
6637 Collector's Encyclopedia of Made in Japan Ceramics, First Ed., White $24.95
5841 Collector's Encyclopedia of Roseville Pottery, Vol. 1, Huxford/Nickel $24.95
5842 Collector's Encyclopedia of Roseville Pottery, Vol. 2, Huxford/Nickel.......$24.95
6646 Collector's Ency. of Stangl Artware, Lamps, and Birds, 2nd Ed., Runge $29.95
6634 Collector's Ultimate Ency. of Hull Pottery, Volume 1, Roberts.........$29.95
6829 The Complete Guide to Corning Ware & Visions Cookware, Coroneos..........$19.95
7530 Decorative Plates, Harran $29.95
5918 Florences' Big Book of Salt & Pepper Shakers $24.95
6320 Gaston's Blue Willow, 3rd Edition $19.95
6630 Gaston's Flow Blue China, The Comprehensive Guide................$29.95
7021 Hansons' American Art Pottery Collection........................$29.95
7032 Head Vases, 2nd Edition, Cole................................$24.95
2379 Lehner's Ency. of U.S. Marks on Pottery, Porcelain & China $24.95
4722 McCoy Pottery Collector's Reference & Value Guide, Hanson/Nissen $19.95
5913 McCoy Pottery, Volume III, Hanson/Nissen $24.95

6835 Meissen Porcelain, Harran...............................$29.95
7536 The Official Precious Moments® Collector's Guide to Figurines, 3rd Ed., Bomm...$19.95
6335 Pictorial Guide to Pottery & Porcelain Marks, Lage $29.95
1440 Red Wing Stoneware, DePasquale/Peck/Peterson $9.95
6838 R.S. Prussia & More, McCaslin $29.95
6945 TV Lamps to Light the World, Shuman $29.95
7043 Uhl Pottery, 2nd Edition, Feldmeyer/Holtzman $16.95
6828 The Ultimate Collector's Encyclopedia of Cookie Jars, Roerig $29.95
6640 Van Patten's ABC's of Collecting Nippon Porcelain................$29.95

OTHER COLLECTIBLES

6446 Antique & Contemporary Advertising Memorabilia, 2nd Edition, Summers $29.95
6935 Antique Golf Collectibles, Georgiady.........................$29.95
1880 Antique Iron, McNerney $9.95
6622 The Art of American Game Calls, Lewis $24.95
6551 The Big Book of Cigarette Lighters, Flanagan $29.95
7024 B.J. Summers' Guide to Coca-Cola, 6th Edition $29.95
1128 Bottle Pricing Guide, 3rd Ed., Cleveland $7.95
6924 Captain John's Fishing Tackle Price Guide, 2nd Edition, Kolbeck..........$24.95
6342 Collectible Soda Pop Memorabilia, Summers $24.95
6625 Collector's Encyclopedia of Bookends, Kuritzky/De Costa $29.95
5666 Collector's Encyclopedia of Granite Ware, Book 2, Greguire $29.95
6928 Early American Furniture, Obbard $19.95
7042 The Ency. of Early American & Antique Sewing Machines, 3rd Ed., Bays $29.95
6561 Field Guide to Fishing Lures, Lewis $16.95
7031 Fishing Lure Collectibles, An Ency. of the Early Years, Murphy/Edmisten $29.95
7350 Flea Market Trader, 16th Edition $15.95
6458 Fountain Pens, Past & Present, 2nd Edition, Erano $24.95
7352 Garage Sale & Flea Market Annual, 15th Edition $19.95
3906 Heywood-Wakefield Modern Furniture, Rouland $18.95
7033 Hot Kitchen & Home Collectibles of the 30s, 40s, and 50s, Zweig $24.95
2216 Kitchen Antiques, 1790 – 1940, McNerney $14.95
7038 The Marketplace Guide to Oak Furniture, 2nd Edition, Blundell $29.95
6639 McDonald's Drinkware, Kelly................................$24.95
6939 Modern Collectible Tins, 2nd Edition, McPherson $24.95
6832 Modern Fishing Lure Collectibles, Volume 4, Lewis $24.95
7349 Modern Fishing Lure Collectibles, Volume 5, Lewis $29.95
6322 Pictorial Guide to Christmas Ornaments & Collectibles, Johnson $29.95
6842 Raycrafts' Americana Price Guide & DVD $19.95
7538 Schroeder's Antiques Price Guide, 26th Edition $17.95
6038 Sewing Tools & Trinkets, Volume 2, Thompson $24.95
5007 Silverplated Flatware, Revised 4th Edition, Hagan $18.95
7367 Star Wars Super Collector's Wish Book, 4th Edition, Carlton $29.95
7537 Summers' Pocket Guide to Coca-Cola, 6th Edition $14.95
6841 Vintage Fabrics, Gridley/Kiplinger/McClure $19.95
6036 Vintage Quilts, Aug/Newman/Roy $24.95
6941 The Wonderful World of Collecting Perfume Bottles, Flanagan $29.95